Advanced Express Web Application Development

Your guide to building professional real-world web applications with Express

Andrew Keig

PUBLISHING

BIRMINGHAM - MUMBAI

Advanced Express Web Application Development

First published: November 2013

Production Reference: 1181113

Published by Packt Publishing Ltd.
Livery Place
35 Livery Street
Birmingham B3 2PB, UK.

ISBN 978-1-78328-249-4

www.packtpub.com

Cover Image by Rima Pawooskar (riima@hotmail.com)

Credits

Author

Andrew Keig

Reviewers

Dave Poon

Artem Vovsya

Acquisition Editors

Erol Staveley

Owen Roberts

Commissioning Editors

Subho Gupta

Sharvari Tawde

Technical Editors

Kapil Hemnani

Tarunveer Shetty

Copy Editors

Sarang Chari

Brandt D'Mello

Lavina Pereira

Project Coordinator

Sherin Padayatty

Proofreader

Simran Bhogal

Indexer

Tejal Daruwale

Production Coordinator

Aparna Bhagat

Cover Work

Aparna Bhagat

About the Author

Andrew Keig is a London based web developer who has been building web applications since 2000. He is the author of Packt's *Instant RabbitMQ Messaging Application Development How-to*. Andrew has a degree in Computing and blogs at blog.airasoul.net on topics he is passionate about, such as Node.js, REST, Web APIs, and behaviour-driven development. He also contributes to various Node.js open source projects. He is a director at Airasoul, which specializes in the design and build of scalable, RESTful, specification-driven, and real-time web-based applications on the Node.js stack. He is also the co-founder of openue.com, a property search startup.

This book is the culmination of my experience working on multiple Node.js projects. I thank those who worked with me: Johnny Hall, Mehdi Avdi, Jozz Hart, Keith Bowditch, Lee Wilson, and Craig Strong.

I would like to thank TJ. Holowaychuk, the author of Express, the author of Node.js, Ryan Dahl, Node's current custodian Isaac Z. Schlueter, and the thousands of Node module developers who have all contributed to making Node.js an awesome space to work in.

Finally, I would also like to thank my reviewers: Dave Poon, and Artem Vovsya for their invaluable input and the team at Packt Publishing for their support.

Finally, thank you to all my family.

About the Reviewers

Dave Poon is a web developer and designer based in Sydney. He started his career as a freelance graphic and web designer in 1998 and worked with web development agencies and medium-size enterprises. After graduating from Central Queensland University with a degree in Multimedia Studies and Master's degree in IT, he began his love affair with Drupal, and worked for a variety of companies that use Drupal.

Currently, he is a Design Lead at Suncorp, one of the biggest financial institutions in Australia. He is also the co-founder of Erlango (`http://erlango.com`), a digital product design startup, located in Sydney and Hong Kong, that creates user-centered digital products and tools for designers and users.

He is also the author of Packt's *Drupal 7 Fields/CCK*.

I would like to thank my wife Rita for her endless patience and support. Without her, what I do would be meaningless.

And also I would like to thank my father for his continued encouragement.

Artem Vovsya has been writing software since 2006, when he started working as a Delphi developer for a little software company. He got his Bachelor's degree in Computer Engineering. He tried his hand at being a Delphi and .NET developer. Two years ago, he fell in love with Node.js, and now he's writing frontend and backend code completely in JavaScript.

Currently he is a frontend developer at Yandex, the leading Russian search engine.

www.PacktPub.com

Support files, eBooks, discount offers and more

You might want to visit www.PacktPub.com for support files and downloads related to your book.

Did you know that Packt offers eBook versions of every book published, with PDF and ePub files available? You can upgrade to the eBook version at www.PacktPub.com and as a print book customer, you are entitled to a discount on the eBook copy. Get in touch with us at service@packtpub.com for more details.

At www.PacktPub.com, you can also read a collection of free technical articles, sign up for a range of free newsletters and receive exclusive discounts and offers on Packt books and eBooks.

http://PacktLib.PacktPub.com

Do you need instant solutions to your IT questions? PacktLib is Packt's online digital book library. Here, you can access, read and search across Packt's entire library of books.

Why Subscribe?

- Fully searchable across every book published by Packt
- Copy and paste, print and bookmark content
- On demand and accessible via web browser

Free Access for Packt account holders

If you have an account with Packt at www.PacktPub.com, you can use this to access PacktLib today and view nine entirely free books. Simply use your login credentials for immediate access.

This book is dedicated to my wife Rima and beloved son Indie.
Thank you both for your love and understanding.

Table of Contents

Preface

Building an Express application that is reliable, robust, maintainable, testable, and can scale beyond a single server requires a bit of extra thought and effort. Express applications that need to survive in a production environment will need to reach out to the *Node* ecosystem and beyond for support. *Advanced Express Web Application Development* aims to deliver a working real-world, single-page application that can meet these goals and allow us the opportunity to explore the more advanced features of Express.

What this book covers

Chapter 1, Foundations, lays the foundation as we put in place a skeleton application; we introduce testing and automation practices that we will use to build our example single-page application.

Chapter 2, Building a Web API, helps in building a web API that our application will consume.

Chapter 3, Templating, helps you create a consuming client with a working web API in place and explore the client- and server-side templating.

Chapter 4, Real-time Communication, helps us to add real-time updates to content displayed in our single-page application.

Chapter 5, Security, guides us to secure our application as we look at authentication, security vulnerabilities, and SSL.

Chapter 6, Scaling, demonstrates scaling our Express application using Redis, and also looks at the benefits of decoupling an Express application.

Chapter 7, Production, examines real-world Express deployment issues such as performance, robustness, and reliability.

What you need for this book

In order to create and run the examples in this book, you will need a Mac or PC running Windows or Linux; you can use any text editor. This book will provide you with instructions on installing Node.js, Express, and various dependencies including Redis and MongoDB.

Who this book is for

If you are an experienced JavaScript developer who wants to build highly scalable, real-world applications using Express, this book is ideal for you. This book is an advanced title and assumes that the reader has some experience with Node.js, JavaScript MVC web development frameworks, and has at least heard of Express before. The reader should also have a basic understanding of Redis and MongoDB. This book is not a tutorial on node but aims to explore some of the more advanced topics you will encounter when developing, deploying, and maintaining an Express web application.

Conventions

In this book, you will find a number of styles of text that distinguish between different kinds of information. Here are some examples of these styles, and an explanation of their meaning.

Code words in text, database table names, folder names, filenames, file extensions, pathnames, dummy URLs, user input, and Twitter handles are shown as follows: "Let's extract our route heartbeat into ./lib/routes/heartbeat.js; the following listing simply exports the route as a function called index:"

A block of code is set as follows:

```
exports.index = function(req, res){
    res.json(200, 'OK');
};
```

Any command-line input or output is written as follows:

```
npm install -g express
NODE_ENV=COVERAGE mocha -R html-cov > coverage.html
```

New terms and **important words** are shown in bold. Words that you see on the screen, in menus or dialog boxes for example, appear in the text like this: "In order to acquire a GitHub token, log in to your GitHub account and go to the **Accounts** section of your **Settings** page, you will need to enter your password. Now click on **Create new token**, name the token if you prefer. Click on the **copy to clipboard** button in order to copy the token into the following **login**."

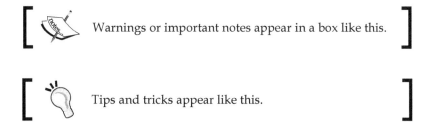

Warnings or important notes appear in a box like this.

Tips and tricks appear like this.

Reader feedback

Feedback from our readers is always welcome. Let us know what you think about this book—what you liked or may have disliked. Reader feedback is important for us to develop titles that you really get the most out of.

To send us general feedback, simply send an e-mail to feedback@packtpub.com, and mention the book title via the subject of your message.

If there is a topic that you have expertise in and you are interested in either writing or contributing to a book, see our author guide on www.packtpub.com/authors.

Customer support

Now that you are the proud owner of a Packt book, we have a number of things to help you to get the most from your purchase.

Downloading the example code

You can download the example code files for all Packt books you have purchased from your account at http://www.packtpub.com. If you purchased this book elsewhere, you can visit http://www.packtpub.com/support and register to have the files e-mailed directly to you.

Errata

Although we have taken every care to ensure the accuracy of our content, mistakes do happen. If you find a mistake in one of our books — maybe a mistake in the text or the code — we would be grateful if you would report this to us. By doing so, you can save other readers from frustration and help us improve subsequent versions of this book. If you find any errata, please report them by visiting http://www.packtpub.com/submit-errata, selecting your book, clicking on the **errata submission form** link, and entering the details of your errata. Once your errata are verified, your submission will be accepted and the errata will be uploaded on our website, or added to any list of existing errata, under the Errata section of that title. Any existing errata can be viewed by selecting your title from http://www.packtpub.com/support.

Piracy

Piracy of copyright material on the Internet is an ongoing problem across all media. At Packt, we take the protection of our copyright and licenses very seriously. If you come across any illegal copies of our works, in any form, on the Internet, please provide us with the location address or website name immediately so that we can pursue a remedy.

Please contact us at copyright@packtpub.com with a link to the suspected pirated material.

We appreciate your help in protecting our authors, and our ability to bring you valuable content.

Questions

You can contact us at questions@packtpub.com if you are having a problem with any aspect of the book, and we will do our best to address it.

1
Foundations

Advanced Express Web Application Development will guide you through the process of building a nontrivial, single-page application using **Express**.

Express is a fast, unopinionated, minimalist, and flexible web application framework for **Node.js** written by TJ. Holowaychuk. It was inspired by **Sinatra**, a web framework for Ruby. Express provides a robust set of features for building single, multi-page, and hybrid web applications and has quickly become the most popular web development framework for node. Express is built on top of an extensible HTTP server framework — also developed by TJ. Holowaychuk — called **Connect**. Connect provides a set of high performance plugins known as middleware. Connect includes over 20 commonly used middleware, including a logger, session support, cookie parser, and more.

This book will guide you through the process of building a single-page application called Vision; a dashboard for software development projects that integrates with GitHub to give you a single-screen snapshot of your software development projects issues and commits. This project will allow us to demonstrate the advanced features Express has to offer and will give us the opportunity to explore the kind of issues encountered in a commercial development and production deployment of a node/Express application.

Feature set

We will now begin the process of building a Vision application. We will start from scratch with a test-first approach. Along the way, we will explore some best practices and offer tips for when developing web applications with node and Express.

The Vision application will include the following features:

```
Feature: Heartbeat
As an administrator
I want to visit an endpoint
So that I can confirm the server is responding

Feature: List projects
As a vision user
I want to see a list of projects
So that I can select a project I want to monitor

Feature: Create project
As a vision user
I want to create a new project
So that I can monitor the activity of multiple repositories

Feature: Get a project
As a vision user
I want to get a project
So that I can monitor the activity of selected repositories

Feature: Edit a project
As a vision user
I want to update a project
So that I can change the repositories I monitor

Feature: Delete a project
As a vision user
I want to delete a project
So that I can remove projects no longer in use

Feature: List repositories
As a vision user
I want to see a list of all repositories for a GitHub account
So that I can select and monitor repositories for my project

Feature: List issues
As a vision user
I want to see a list of multiple repository issues in real time
So that I can review and fix issues

Feature: List commits
As a vision user
```

```
I want to see a list of multiple repository commits in real time
So that I can review those commits

Feature: Master Page
As a vision user
I want the vision application served as a single page
So that I can spend less time waiting for page loads

Feature: Authentication
As a vision user
I want to be able to authenticate via Github
So that I can view project activity
```

The following screenshot is of our Vision application; it contains a list of projects, repositories, commits, and issues. The upper-right corner has a login link that we will use for authentication:

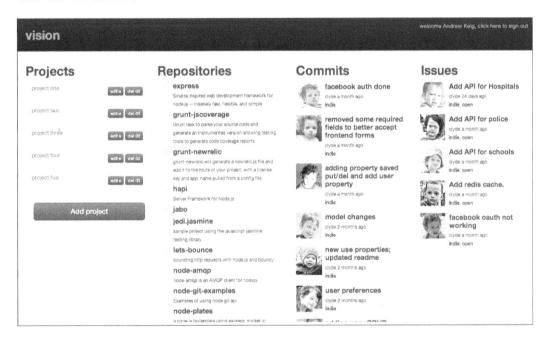

Installation

If you do not have node installed, visit: `http://nodejs.org/download/`.

There is also an installation guide on the node GitHub repository wiki if you prefer not to or cannot use an installer: `https://github.com/joyent/node/wiki/Installation`.

Let's install Express globally:

```
npm install -g express
```

 Download the source code for this book here: `https://github.com/AndrewKeig/advanced-express-application-development`.

If you have downloaded the source code, install its dependencies by running this command:

```
npm install
```

package.json

Let's start by creating a root project folder called `vision` and add a `package.json` file to it: `./package.json`:

```json
{
  "name": "chapter-1",
  "version": "0.0.0",
  "private": true,
  "scripts": {
    "start": "node app.js"
  }
  "dependencies": {
    "express": "3.x"
  }
}
```

 Downloading the example code

You can download the example code files for all Packt books you have purchased from your account at `http://www.packtpub.com`. If you purchased this book elsewhere, you can visit `http://www.packtpub.com/support` and register to have the files e-mailed directly to you.

Testing Express with Mocha and SuperTest

Now that we have Express installed and our `package.json` file in place, we can begin to drive out our application with a test-first approach. We will now install two modules to assist us: `mocha` and `supertest`.

Mocha is a testing framework for node; it's flexible, has good async support, and allows you to run tests in both a TDD and BDD style. It can also be used on both the client and server side. Let's install Mocha with the following command:

```
npm install -g mocha --save-dev
```

SuperTest is an integration testing framework that will allow us to easily write tests against a RESTful HTTP server. Let's install SuperTest:

```
npm install supertest --save-dev
```

Feature: Heartbeat

```
As an administrator
I want to visit an endpoint
So that I can confirm the server is responding
```

Let's add a test to `./test/heartbeat.js` for our `Heartbeat` feature. This resource will get a status from the route `/heartbeat` and return a `200 Ok` status code. Let's write our first integration test using Mocha and SuperTest. First off, create a folder named `/test` inside your `vision` folder.

Our test describes `heartbeat`; it expects the response to have a JSON content type and a status code equal to `200 Ok`.

```
var app = require('../app')
, request = require('supertest');

describe('vision heartbeat api', function(){
  describe('when requesting resource /heartbeat', function(){
    it('should respond with 200', function(done){
      request(app)
      .get('/heartbeat')
      .expect('Content-Type', /json/)
      .expect(200, done);
    });
  });
});
```

Let's implement the Heartbeat feature; we start by creating a simple Express server, ./lib/express/index.js. We include the express and http modules and create an Express application. We then add an application setting via app.set called port and set it to 3000. We define a /heartbeat route via app.get with which we pass a request handler, function, that takes two parameters: req (request) and res (response). We use the response object to return a JSON response. We create an HTTP server with http.createServer by passing our Express application to it; we listen on port 3000 as defined in our application setting called port. We then export the application with module.exports; exporting the application allows us to test it.

```
var express = require('express')
  , http = require('http')
  , app = express();

app.set('port', 3000);

app.get('/heartbeat', function(req, res){
  res.json(200, 'OK')
});

http.createServer(app).listen(app.get('port'));
module.exports = app;
```

We now create ./app.js in the root of our project and export the express module:

```
module.exports = require('./lib/express');
```

To run our test, execute the following command:

```
mocha
```

You should then receive the response:

```
1 tests complete (14 ms)
```

If successful, try running the application by executing this command:

```
npm start
```

With the app running, run the following curl command in a new terminal and you can see our heartbeat JSON response return a 200 Ok status code:

```
curl -i http://127.0.0.1:3000/heartbeat
```

```
HTTP/1.1 200 OK
X-Powered-By: Express
```

```
Content-Type: application/json; charset=utf-8

Content-Length: 4

Date: Fri, 14 Jun 2013 08:28:50 GMT

Connection: keep-alive
```

Continuous testing with Mocha

One of the great things about working with a dynamic language and one of the things that has drawn me to node is the ability to easily do **Test-Driven Development** and continuous testing. Simply run Mocha with the -w watch switch and Mocha will respond when changes to our codebase are made, and will automatically rerun the tests:

```
mocha -w
```

Code coverage with Mocha and JSCoverage

Mocha is able to generate a code coverage report with a little help from **JSCoverage**. Install JSCoverage for your environment from http://siliconforks.com/jscoverage/. JSCoverage will parse source code and generate an instrumented version; this enables mocha to execute this generated code and create a report. We will need to update ./app.js.

```
module.exports = (process.env['NODE_ENV'] === "COVERAGE")
  ? require('./lib-cov/express')
  : require('./lib/express');
```

JSCoverage takes as arguments an input directory, and an output directory:

```
jscoverage lib lib-cov
```

Depending on your version of JSCoverage, you may need to add the -no-highlight switch:

```
jscoverage lib lib-cov --no-highlight
```

The following command will generate the coverage report, as shown in the following screenshot:

```
NODE_ENV=COVERAGE mocha -R html-cov > coverage.html
```

Configuring Express with Nconf

Nconf is a configuration tool that we will use to create hierarchical/environment configuration files for our application. Let's install Nconf:

```
npm install nconf --save
```

The first thing we will do is to move the following hardcoded port number from our Express application into our configuration:

```
app.set('port', 3000);
```

Let's create the module `./lib/configuration/index.js`, which will allow us to to read configuration data from JSON files. We import the `nconf` module and define a constructor function, `Config`. We then load a configuration file based on the current environment and load the default configuration that holds non-environmental configuration data. We also define a function `get(key)`, which accepts a key and returns a value. We will use this function to read configuration data:

```
var nconf = require('nconf');

function Config(){
```

```
    nconf.argv().env("_");
    var environment = nconf.get("NODE:ENV") || "development";
    nconf.file(environment, "config/" + environment + ".json");
    nconf.file("default", "config/default.json");
}

Config.prototype.get = function(key) {
  return nconf.get(key);
};

module.exports = new Config();
```

Let's write some configuration for our application. Add the following default configuration to `./config/default.json`; this will be shared amongst all environments:

```
{
  "application": {
    "name": "vision"
  }
}
```

Now add the following configuration to the development, test, and coverage config files: `./config/development.json`, `./config/test.json`, and `./config/coverage.json`.

```
{
  "express": {
    "port": 3000
  }
}
```

Let's change our Express server `./lib/express/index.js` so that it reads `express:port` from configuration:

```
var express = require('express')
  , http = require('http')
  , config = require('../configuration')
  , app = express();

app.set('port', config.get("express:port"));

app.get('/hearbeat', function(req, res){
  res.json(200, 'OK');
});

http.createServer(app).listen(app.get('port'));

module.exports = app;
```

Extracting routes

Express supports multiple options for application structure. Extracting elements of an Express application into separate files is one option; a good candidate for this is routes.

Let's extract our route heartbeat into `./lib/routes/heartbeat.js`; the following listing simply exports the route as a function called `index`:

```
exports.index = function(req, res){
  res.json(200, 'OK');
};
```

Let's make a change to our Express server and remove the anonymous function we pass to `app.get` for our route and replace it with a call to the function in the following listing. We import the route `heartbeat` and pass in a callback function, `heartbeat.index`:

```
var express = require('express')
  , http = require('http')
  , config = require('../configuration')
  , heartbeat = require('../routes/heartbeat')
  , app = express();

app.set('port', config.get('express:port'));
app.get('/heartbeat', heartbeat.index);

http.createServer(app).listen(app.get('port'));
module.exports = app;
```

404 handling middleware

In order to handle a `404 Not Found` response, let's add a 404 not found middleware. Let's write a test, `./test/heartbeat.js`; the content type returned should be JSON and the status code expected should be `404 Not Found`:

```
describe('vision heartbeat api', function(){
  describe('when requesting resource /missing', function(){
    it('should respond with 404', function(done){
      request(app)
      .get('/missing')
      .expect('Content-Type', /json/)
      .expect(404, done);
    })
  });
});
```

Now, add the following middleware to `./lib/middleware/notFound.js`. Here we export a function called `index` and call `res.json`, which returns a 404 status code and the message `Not Found`. The next parameter is not called as our 404 middleware ends the request by returning a response. Calling next would call the next middleware in our Express stack; we do not have any more middleware due to this, it's customary to add error middleware and 404 middleware as the last middleware in your server:

```
exports.index = function(req, res, next){
    res.json(404, 'Not Found.');
};
```

Now add the 404 not found middleware to `./lib/express/index.js`:

```
var express = require('express')
  , http = require('http')
  , config = require('../configuration')
  , heartbeat = require('../routes/heartbeat')
  , notFound = require('../middleware/notFound')
  , app = express();

app.set('port', config.get('express:port'));
app.get('/heartbeat', heartbeat.index);
app.use(notFound.index);

http.createServer(app).listen(app.get('port'));
module.exports = app;
```

Logging middleware

Express comes with a logger middleware via Connect; it's very useful for debugging an Express application. Let's add it to our Express server `./lib/express/index.js`:

```
var express = require('express')
  , http = require('http')
  , config = require('../configuration')
  , heartbeat = require('../routes/heartbeat')
  , notFound = require('../middleware/notFound')
  , app = express();

app.set('port', config.get('express:port'));
app.use(express.logger({ immediate: true, format: 'dev' }));
app.get('/heartbeat', heartbeat.index);
```

```
app.use(notFound.index);

http.createServer(app).listen(app.get('port'));
module.exports = app;
```

The `immediate` option will write a log line on request instead of on response. The `dev` option provides concise output colored by the response status. The logger middleware is placed high in the Express stack in order to log all requests.

Logging with Winston

We will now add logging to our application using **Winston**; let's install Winston:

```
npm install winston --save
```

The 404 middleware will need to log 404 not found, so let's create a simple logger module, `./lib/logger/index.js`; the details of our logger will be configured with Nconf. We import Winston and the configuration modules. We define our `Logger` function, which constructs and returns a file logger — `winston.transports.File` — that we configure using values from our `config`. We default the loggers maximum size to 1 MB, with a maximum of three rotating files. We instantiate the `Logger` function, returning it as a singleton.

```
var winston = require('winston')
  , config = require('../configuration');

function Logger(){
  return winston.add(winston.transports.File, {
    filename: config.get('logger:filename'),
    maxsize: 1048576,
    maxFiles: 3,
    level: config.get('logger:level')
  });
}

module.exports = new Logger();
```

Let's add the `Logger` configuration details to our config files `./config/development.json` and `./config/test.json`:

```
{
  "express": {
    "port": 3000
  },
  "logger" : {
```

```
    "filename": "logs/run.log",
    "level": "silly",
  }
}
```

Let's alter the ./lib/middleware/notFound.js middleware to log errors. We import our logger and log an error message via logger when a 404 Not Found response is thrown:

```
var logger = require("../logger");

exports.index = function(req, res, next){
  logger.error('Not Found');
  res.json(404, 'Not Found');
};
```

Task automation with Grunt

Grunt is a task runner and a great way to automate your node projects. Let's add a simple grunt script to our project in order to automate running tests and code coverage. Let's install Grunt and Grunt CLI:

```
npm install -g grunt-cli
npm install grunt --save-dev
```

The grunt-cafe-mocha is a grunt module for running mocha; this module will also allow us to automate code coverage reports:

```
npm install grunt-cafe-mocha --save-dev
```

The grunt-jscoverage simply generates an instrumented version of our source code and writes it to ./lib-cov:

```
npm install grunt-jscoverage --save-dev
```

The grunt-env allows you to set the current node environment, NODE_ENV:

```
npm install grunt-env  --save-dev
```

Let's create a grunt file ./gruntfile.js. We load the grunt modules we just installed, and grunt.initConfig contains a configuration for each grunt module:

```
module.exports = function(grunt) {
  grunt.loadNpmTasks('grunt-jscoverage');
  grunt.loadNpmTasks('grunt-cafe-mocha');
```

```
    grunt.loadNpmTasks('grunt-env');

    grunt.initConfig({
      env: {
        test: { NODE_ENV: 'TEST' },
        coverage: { NODE_ENV: 'COVERAGE' }
      },
      cafemocha: {
        test: {
          src: 'test/*.js',
          options: {
            ui: 'bdd',
            reporter: 'spec',
          },
        },
        coverage: {
          src: 'test/*.js',
          options: {
            ui: 'bdd',
            reporter: 'html-cov',
            coverage: {
              output: 'coverage.html'
            }
          }
        },
      },
      jscoverage: {
        options: {
          inputDirectory: 'lib',
          outputDirectory: 'lib-cov',
          highlight: false
        }
      }
    });
    grunt.registerTask('test', [ 'env:test', 'cafemocha:test' ]);
    grunt.registerTask('coverage', [ 'env:coverage',
      'jscoverage', 'cafemocha:coverage' ]);
};
```

The configuration for `cafemocha` contains two sections; one for running our tests and one for generating a code coverage report. In order to run our tests from grunt, execute the following command:

`grunt test`

The following line registers a task that sets the environment using `env` and runs both the `jscoverage` and `cafemocha:coverage` tasks in sequence:

```
grunt.registerTask('coverage', [ 'env:coverage',
    'jscoverage', 'cafemocha:coverage' ]);
```

In order to run our coverage from grunt, execute the following command:

`grunt coverage`

This command will generate the coverage report as described earlier.

Summary

We have put in place a fairly solid framework for developing our Vision project; we have implemented a simple feature, heartbeat, which when visited, simply informs us whether our Express server is up and running. We have automated various development tasks, such as running tests and creating code coverage reports. We also have in place some logging using Winston. In the next chapter, we will implement a web API.

2
Building a Web API

With the foundations in place, we begin the process of building a Web API for our Vision project. We will start by setting up a persistence layer using MongoDB. We will then implement, feature-by-feature, the various aspects of our Web API.

Persisting data with MongoDB and Mongoose

MongoDB is an open source document-oriented database system. MongoDB stores structured data such as JSON-like documents, simplifying integration.

Let's start by creating a MongoDB schema for our project. The schema contains some basic information related to the project such as the project's name, a GitHub access token, a user, and a list of repositories.

Let's install Mongoose, a MongoDB Object Document Mapper for Node.js; it provides a schema-based solution to modeling your data.

```
npm install mongoose --save
```

Let's configure our application to use MongoDB and Mongoose; we add a URL for MongoDB to our configuration files `./lib/config/*.js`:

```
{
  "express": {
    "port": 3000
  },
  "logger" : {
    "filename": "logs/run.log",
    "level": "silly"
  },
```

```
  "mongo": {
    "url":   "mongodb://localhost/vision"
  }
}
```

Let's create a MongoDB connection module, ./lib/db/index.js, which simply pulls in the MongoDB URL from our Winston configuration and opens a connection:

```
var mongoose = require('mongoose')
, config = require('../configuration')
, connectionString = config.get("mongo:url")
, options = { server: { auto_reconnect: true, poolSize: 10 } };

mongoose.connection.open(connectionString, options);
```

We now create a model class ./lib/models/index.js that defines our ProjectSchema:

```
var mongoose = require('mongoose'),
    Schema = mongoose.Schema;

var ProjectSchema = new Schema({
    name         : { type: String, required: true, index: true }
  , token        : { type: String }
  , user         : { type: String, required: true, index: true }
  , created      : { type: Date, default: Date.now }
  , repositories : [ { type: String } ]
});

mongoose.model('Project', ProjectSchema);
module.exports = mongoose;
```

In order to run the following examples, we need a running instance of MongoDB. You can download MongoDB from http://www.mongodb.org. Run the following command to start MongoDB:

```
mongod
```

GitHub tokens

In order to acquire a GitHub token, log in to your GitHub account and go to the **Accounts** section of your **Settings** page. Here you will need to enter your password. Now click on **Create new token**, and name the token, if you prefer. Click on the **copy to clipboard** button in order to copy the token into the following login file.

Let's create a `login` file— `./test/login.js` —with the data from GitHub. We will use this in order to call the GitHub API; this will be removed in a later chapter.

```
module.exports = {
  user : '#USER#'
  token : '#TOKEN#'
}
```

Feature: Create a project

```
As a vision user
I want to create a new project
So that I can monitor the activity of multiple repositories
```

Let's add a test to our existing set of tests for our feature `Create a project`. This resource will POST a project to the route `/project` and return a `201 Created` status code. The following test: `./test/project.js` is the `201 Created` test.

 This book will not document the full set of tests for a feature. Please refer to the source code for the full set of tests.

In this example, SuperTest executes an `end` function that returns a response; this allows us to check the headers and body of the response.

```
describe('when creating a new resource /project', function(){
  var project = {
    name: "new project"
    , user: login.user
    , token: login.token
    , repositories    : [ "12345", "9898" ]
  };

  it('should respond with 201', function(done){
    request(app)
    .post('/project')
    .send(project)
    .expect('Content-Type', /json/)
    .expect(201)
    .end(function (err, res) {
      var proj = JSON.parse(res.text);
      assert.equal(proj.name, project.name);
      assert.equal(proj.user, login.user);
```

```
          assert.equal(proj.token, login.token);
          assert.equal(proj.repositories[0],
            project.repositories[0]);
          assert.equal(proj.repositories[1],
            project.repositories[1]);
          assert.equal(res.header['location'],
            '/project/' + proj._id);
          done();
          });
        });
      });
```

In order for some of our tests to work, we will need some test data. So, the following `./test/project.js` will tear down any existing project data and add a new project using a Mocha hook `beforeEach`, that runs before each test:

```
    beforeEach(function(done){
      mongoose.connection.collections['projects'].
        drop( function(err) {
      var proj = {
        name: "test name"
        , user: login.user
        , token: login.token
        , repositories   : [ "node-plates" ]
      };

      mongoose.connection.collections['projects'].insert(proj,
        function(err, docs) {
          id = docs[0]._id;
          done();
        });
      });
    })
```

Let's install `string.js`, a lightweight JavaScript library that provides extra string methods. This will help us validate a request:

npm install string --save

Let's implement the `Create a project` feature. We start by creating a `Project` module `./lib/project/index.js`. We import a Mongoose schema for the `Project` model and define a function called `post`, which accepts the `name` and `data` as arguments. We call the static function `Project.findOne` to check if the project exists, and if the project is unique, we call the `project.save` function, which saves the project.

```
var ProjectSchema =
  require('../models').model('Project');

function Project() {};

Project.prototype.post = function(name, data, callback){
  var query = {'name': name};
  var project = new ProjectSchema(data);

  ProjectSchema.findOne(query, function(error, proj) {
    if (error) return callback(error, null);
    if (proj != null) return callback(null, null);

    project.save(function (error, p) {
      if (error) return callback(error, null);
      return callback(null, p);
    });
  });
};
```

Let's add a new route `./lib/routes/project.js`. We import a `logger` variable, a `ProjectService` module, and define a route called `Post`, that uses `req.body` to gain access to the items we POST in a request. We then validate the request that returns a `400 Bad Request` if it is invalid. If the request is valid, we add the user and the token to the body and call `Project.post`; if we get an error, we return `500 Internal Server Error`, and if the project already exists, we return a `409 Conflict` response. If the request is ok, we set `res.location` on the response for our new resource and return a `201 Created` response:

```
var logger = require("../logger")
, S = require('string')
, login = require('../../test/login')
, ProjectService = require('../project')
, Project = new ProjectService();

exports.post = function(req, res){
  logger.info('Post.' + req.body.name);

  if (S(req.body.name).isEmpty() )
  return res.json(400, 'Bad Request');

  req.body.user = login.user;
  req.body.token = login.token;
```

```
    Project.post(req.body.name, req.body, function(error, project) {
        if (error) return res.json(500, 'Internal Server Error');
        if (project == null) return res.json(409, 'Conflict');
        res.location('/project/' +  project._id);
        return res.json(201, project);
    });
};
```

In order to add our new route and allow our application to support HTTP POST, we need to make a few changes to our Express server `./lib/express/index.js`.

First, we import the `db` module we created at the beginning of this chapter, which opens a connection to a MongoDB database. We then import the `project` route module we just created. Importantly, `app.use(express.bodyParser())` parses the request body when the forms are submitted. The `bodyParser` middleware supports `application/x-www-form-urlencoded`, `application/json`, and `multipart/form-data`. We add a new route at `/project` for posting a project.

```
var express = require('express')
  , http = require('http')
  , config = require('../configuration')
  , db = require('../db')
  , heartbeat = require('../routes/heartbeat')
  , project = require('../routes/project')
  , error = require('../routes/error')
  , notFound = require('../middleware/notFound')
  , app = express();

app.use(express.bodyParser());
app.set('port', config.get('express:port'));
app.use(express.logger({ immediate: true, format: 'dev' }));
app.get('/heartbeat', heartbeat.index);
app.post('/project', project.post);
app.use(notFound.index);

http.createServer(app).listen(app.get('port'));
module.exports = app;
```

Feature: Get a project

```
As a vision user
I want to get a project
So that I can monitor the activity of selected repositories
```

Let's add a test to the existing set of tests `./test/project.js` for our feature `Get a project`. This resource will GET a project from route `/project/:id`, and return a `200 OK` status.

Let's install `underscore.js`; a utility-belt library that provides functional programming support:

`npm install underscore --save`

```
describe('when requesting an available resource /project/:id',
  function(){
  it('should respond with 200', function(done){
    request(app)
    .get('/project/' + id)
    .expect('Content-Type', /json/)
    .expect(200)
    .end(function (err, res) {
      var proj = JSON.parse(res.text);
      assert.equal(proj._id, id);
      assert(_.has(proj, '_id'));
      assert(_.has(proj, 'name'));
      assert(_.has(proj, 'user'));
      assert(_.has(proj, 'token'));
      assert(_.has(proj, 'created'));
      assert(_.has(proj, 'repositories'));
      done();
    });
  });
});
```

Let's implement the `Get a project` feature `./lib/project/index.js` and add a `get` function. We attempt to retrieve a project by calling the static function `Project.findOne`. If we get an error, we return it, if we find the project then we return the project:

```
Project.prototype.get = function(id, callback){
  var query = {"_id" : id};

  ProjectSchema.findOne(query, function(error, project) {
    if (error) return callback(error, null);
    return callback(null, project);
  });
};
```

Let's add a new route `./lib/routes/project.js`. We start by defining a route called `get`. We validate the request using a regular expression for a valid Mongoose `ObjectId`; and it returns a `400 Bad Request` status if the request is invalid. We attempt to retrieve a project by calling `Project.get` passing the `id`. If we get an error, we return `500 Internal Server Error`; if the project does not exist, we return a `404 Not Found`. If we find the project, we return the project and a `200 OK` response:

```
exports.get = function(req, res){
  logger.info('Request.' + req.url);

  Project.get(req.params.id, function(error, project) {
    if (error) return res.json(500, 'Internal Server Error');
    if (project == null) return res.json(404, 'Not Found');
    return res.json(200, project);
  });
};
```

Now add the following route to `./lib/express/index.js`:

```
app.get('/project/:id', project.get);
```

Feature: Edit a project

```
As a vision user
I want to update a project
So that I can change the repositories I monitor
```

Let's add a test to our existing set of tests `./test/project.js` for our `Edit a project` feature. This resource will PUT a project to route `/project/:id`, and return a `204 No Content` status:

```
describe('when updating an existing resource /project/:id',
  function(){
  var project = {
    name: "new test name"
    , user: login.user
    , token: login.token
    , repositories    : [ "12345", "9898" ]
  };

  it('should respond with 204', function(done){

    request(app)
    .put('/project/' + id)
```

```
    .send(project)
    .expect(204, done);
  });
});
```

Let's implement the `Edit a project` feature `./lib/project/index.js` and add a `put` function. We attempt to retrieve a project by calling the static function `Project.findOne`. If we get an error, we return it; if we cannot find the project, we return null. If we find the project, we update it and return the project:

```
Project.prototype.put = function(id, update, callback){
  var query = {"_id": id};
  delete update._id;

  ProjectSchema.findOne(query, function(error, project) {
    if (error) return callback(error, null);
    if (project == null) return callback(null, null);

    ProjectSchema.update(query, update, function(error, project) {
      if (error) return callback(error, null);
      return callback(null, {});
    });
  });
};
```

Let's add a new route `./lib/routes/project.js`. We start by defining a route called `put`, we then validate the request by returning a `400 Bad Request` if the request is invalid. We add a login user and token to the body of the request; this will be removed in a later chapter. We attempt to update the project by calling `Project.put` passing the `id`. If we get an error, we return `500 Internal Server Error`; if the project does not exist, we return a `404 Not Found` status. If we find the project, then we return a `204 No Content` response:

```
exports.put = function(req, res){
  logger.info('Put.' + req.params.id);

  if (S(req.body.name).isEmpty() )
  return res.json(400, 'Bad Request');

  req.body.user = login.user;
  req.body.token = login.token;

  Project.put(req.params.id, req.body, function(error, project) {
    if (error) return res.json(500, 'Internal Server Error');
```

```
    if (project == null) return res.json(404, 'Not Found');
    return res.json(204, 'No Content');
  });
};
```

Now, add the following route to the Express server `./lib/express/index.js`:

```
app.put('/project/:id', project.put);
```

Feature: Delete a project

```
As a vision user
I want to delete a project
So that I can remove projects no longer in use
```

Let's add a test to `./test/project.js` for our feature `Delete a project`. This resource will DELETE a project at route `/project/:id` and return a `204 No Content` status:

```
describe('when deleting an existing resource /project/:id',
  function(){
  it('should respond with 204', function(done){
    request(app)
    .del('/project/' + id)
    .expect(204, done);
  });
});
```

Let's implement the `Delete a project` feature `./lib/project/index.js` and add a `del` function. We attempt to delete a project by calling the static function `Project.findOne`. If we get an error, we return it; if we cannot find the project, we return `null`. If we find the project, we delete it and return an empty response.

```
Project.prototype.del = function(id, callback){
  var query = {'_id': id};

  ProjectSchema.findOne(query, function(error, project) {
    if (error) return callback(error, null);
    if (project == null) return callback(null, null);

    project.remove(function (error) {
      if (error) return callback(error, null);
      return callback(null, {});
    });
  });
};
```

Let's add a new route `./lib/routes/project.js`. We start by defining a route called `del`. We attempt to delete the project by calling `Project.del` and passing the id. If we get an error, we return `500 Internal Server Error`; if the project does not exist, we return a `404 Not Found`. If we find the project, we return a `204 No Content` response.

```
exports.del = function(req, res){
  logger.info('Delete.' + req.params.id);

  Project.del(req.params.id, function(error, project) {
    if (error) return res.json(500, 'Internal Server Error');
    if (project == null) return res.json(404, 'Not Found');
    return res.json(204, 'No Content');
  });
};
```

Now, add the following route to the Express server `./lib/express/index.js`:

```
app.del('/project/:id', project.del);
```

Feature: List projects

```
As a vision user
I want to see a list of projects
So that I can select a project I want to monitor
```

Let's add a test to `./test/project.js` for our feature `List projects`. This resource will GET all projects from route `/project` and return a `200 Ok` status.

```
describe('when requesting resource get all projects', function(){
  it('should respond with 200', function(done){
    request(app)
    .get('/project/?user=' + login.user)
    .expect('Content-Type', /json/)
    .expect(200)
    .end(function (err, res) {
      var proj = _.first(JSON.parse(res.text))
      assert(_.has(proj, '_id'));
      assert(_.has(proj, 'name'));
      assert(_.has(proj, 'user'));
      assert(_.has(proj, 'token'));
      assert(_.has(proj, 'created'));
      assert(_.has(proj, 'repositories'));
      done();
```

```
      });
    });
  });
```

Let's implement the `List projects` feature `./lib/project/index.js` and add an `all` function. We attempt to retrieve all projects by calling the static function `Project.find` and querying by a user `id`. If we get an error we return it, if we find the projects, we return the projects:

```
Project.prototype.all = function(id, callback){
  var query = {"user" : id};

  ProjectSchema.find(query, function(error, projects) {
    if (error) return callback(error, null);
    return callback(null, projects);
  });
};
```

Let's add a new route `./lib/routes/project.js`. We start by defining a route called `all`. We start by retrieving a users `id`. In order to accommodate the fact that we have not implemented an authentication strategy; we get the user details from our hard-coded `login.user` object. We will clean this up in a future chapter. We attempt to retrieve a project by calling `Project.all`, passing the `userId`. If we get an error, we return `500 Internal Server Error`; if we find projects, we return the projects and a `200 OK` response.

```
exports.all = function(req, res){
  logger.info('Request.' + req.url);

  var userId = login.user || req.query.user || req.user.id;

  Project.all(userId, function(error, projects) {
    if (error) return res.json(500, 'Internal Server Error');
    if (projects == null) projects = {};
    return res.json(200, projects);
  });
};
```

Now, add the following route to the Express server `./lib/express/index.js`:

```
app.get('/project', project.all);
```

GitHub API

Our project API is complete but things are about to get a little more complicated as we attempt to communicate with the GitHub API. Let's install the following modules.

The `github` module provides an object-oriented wrapper for the GitHub v3 API; the complete API for this module can be found at `http://mikedeboer.github.io/node-github/`.

```
npm install github --save
```

The `async` module is a utility module that provides around 20 powerful functions for working with asynchronous JavaScript. The `async` module is a control-flow module and will allow us to do operations over IO in a clean, controlled way.

```
npm install async --save
```

The `moment.js` is a library for parsing, validating, manipulating, and formatting dates.

```
npm install moment --save
```

Feature: List repositories

```
As a vision user
I want to see a list of all repositories for a GitHub account
So that I can select and monitor repositories for my project
```

Let's add a test to `./test/github.js` for our feature `List repositories`. This resource will GET all repositories for a project from the route `project/:id/repos` and return a `200 Ok` status:

```
describe('when requesting an available resource
  /project/:id/repos', function(){
  it('should respond with 200', function(done){
    this.timeout(5000);
    request(app)
    .get('/project/' + id + '/repos/')
    .expect('Content-Type', /json/)
    .expect(200)
    .end(function (err, res) {
      var repo = _.first(JSON.parse(res.text))
      assert(_.has(repo, 'id'));
      assert(_.has(repo, 'name'));
      assert(_.has(repo, 'description'));
      done();
```

```
      });
    });
  });
```

The first thing we need to do is create a `GitHubRepo` module in `./lib/github/index.js`. We start by importing the required modules including `github`. We define a constructor function that accepts as input a GitHub access `token` and a `user`. We then instantiate a `GitHubApi` module, calling `github.authenticate`, which authenticates based on the token:

```
var GitHubApi = require("github")
, config = require('../configuration')
, async =  require("async")
, moment = require('moment')
, _ =  require("underscore")

function GitHubRepo(token, user) {
  this.token = token;
  this.user = user;

  this.github = new GitHubApi({
    version: "3.0.0",
    timeout: 5000 });

  this.github.authenticate({
    type: "oauth",
    token: token
  });
};

module.exports = GitHubRepo;
```

Let's implement the feature `List repositories` and add it to our new `GitHubRepo` module in `./lib/github/index.js`. We start by defining our prototype function `repositories`. We call `getAll` on the `github` module. If we get an error, we return the error; if no repositories are found we return a `null` value. If we find repositories, we use the `map` function to create a new array of items using the `underscore pick` function to select the three attributes `id`, `name`, and `description`. We return these items **via** `callback`:

```
GitHubRepo.prototype.repositories = function(callback) {
  this.github.repos.getAll({}, function(error, response) {
    if (error) return callback(error, null);
    if (response == null) return callback(null, null);
```

```
      var items = response.map(function(model) {
        return _.pick(model, ['id','name', 'description']);
      });

      callback(null, items);
    });
  };
```

Let's add a `repos` function to `./lib/project/index.js`. We start by importing the `GitHubRepo` module and we attempt to retrieve the project by calling the static function `Project.findOne`. If we get an error, we return the error; if the project does not exist we return a `null` value. If we find the project, we create a `GithubRepo` module and initialize it with a `token` and a `user`, and assign it to `git`. We then call `git.repositories` which returns a response. If we get an error, we return an `error`, if we do not find any repositories, we return a `null` value. If we find repositories, we use the `map` function to create a new array of items using `underscore pick` function to select three attributes, including `id`, `name`, and `description`. We add a fourth attribute, `enabled`, which signifies if our project has the repository assigned to it and returns all the repositories:

```
  , GitHubRepo = require('../github')

  Project.prototype.repos = function(id, callback){
    ProjectSchema.findOne({_id: id}, function(error, project) {
      if (error) return callback(error, null);
      if (project == null) return callback(null, null);

      var git = new GitHubRepo(project.token, project.user);

      git.repositories(function(error, response){
        if (error) return callback(error, null);
        if (response == null) return callback("error", null);

        items = response.map(function(model) {
          var item = _.pick(model, ['id','name',
            'description''description']);
          var enabled = _.find(project.repositories, function(p)
            { return p == item.name; });
          (enabled) ? item.enabled = 'checked' : item.enabled = '';
          return item;
        });

        return callback(null, items);
      });
    });
  };
```

Let's add a new route `repos` to `./lib/routes/github.js`. We instantiate a new `ProjectService` and then attempt to retrieve the projects repositories by calling the function `Project.repos`. If we get an error, we return `500 Internal Server Error`. If no repositories are returned, we return a `404 Not Found` status. If we receive repositories, we return a `200 OK` status with the repositories.

```
, ProjectService = require('../project')
, Project = new ProjectService();

exports.repos = function(req, res){
  logger.info('Request.' + req.url);

  Project.repos(req.params.id, function(error, repos) {
    if (error) return res.json(500, 'Internal Server Error');
    if (repos == null) return res.json(404, 'Not Found');
    return res.json(200, repos);
  });
};
```

Now, add the following route to `./lib/express/index.js`:

```
app.get('/project/:id/repos', github.repos);
```

Feature: List commits

```
As a vision user
I want to see a list of multiple repository commits in real time
So that I can review those commits
```

Let's add a test to `./test/github.js` for our `List commits` feature. This resource will GET the 10 most recent commits for all repositories in a project via the route `project/:id/commits` and return a `200 OK` status:

```
describe('when requesting an available resource
  /project/:id/commits', function(){
  it('should respond with 200', function(done){
    this.timeout(5000);
    request(app)
    .get('/project/' + id + '/commits')
    .expect('Content-Type', /json/)
    .expect(200)
    .end(function (err, res) {
      var commit = _.first(JSON.parse(res.text))
      assert(_.has(commit, 'message'));
      assert(_.has(commit, 'date'));
```

```
          assert(_.has(commit, 'login'));
          assert(_.has(commit, 'avatar_url'));
          assert(_.has(commit, 'ago'));
          assert(_.has(commit, 'repository'));
          done();
      });
    });
  });
```

Let's implement the `List commits` feature, and add it to our new `GitHubRepo` module in `./lib/github/index.js`. We start by defining our function, `commits`, that takes a list of `repos`. We use `async.each` to loop though all `repos`. The `async` module allows us to do asynchronous work over IO.

We then call `github.repos.getCommits`; we pass it our GitHub `user` and `repo`. We call the `callback` if `github.repos.getCommits()` returns an error. When we get a response, we use the `map` function to create a new array of items using the `uderscore` `pick` function to select two attributes: `committer` and `message`. If the item has a `committer`, we use underscores the `extend` function and add the committers, `login` and `avatar_url`. We return the items to the main function via `callback` and use underscores `sort` function to sort the items by date and select the top 10 items. We then return the commits via `callback`:

```
GitHubRepo.prototype.commits = function(repos, callback) {
  var me = this;
  var items = [];

  async.each(repos, function(repo, callback) {
    me.github.repos.getCommits({ user: me.user,
      repo: repo }, function(error, response) {
      if (error) return callback();
      if (response == null) return callback();

      var repoItems = response.map(function(model) {
        var item =_.pick(model.commit, ['message']);
        if (model.commit.committer) _.extend(item,
          _.pick(model.commit.committer, ['date']));
        if (model.committer) _.extend(item,
          _.pick(model.committer, ['login', 'avatar_url']));
        item.ago = moment(item.date).fromNow();
        item.repository  = repo;
        return item;
      });
```

```
        items = _.union(items, repoItems);
        callback(null, items );
      });
    }
    , function(error) {
      var top = _.chain(items)
      .sortBy(function(item){ return item.date })
      .reverse()
      .first(10)
      .value();

      callback(error, top);
    });
  };
```

Let's add a `commits` function to `./lib/project/index.js`. We start by defining a function called `commits`. We attempt to retrieve the project by calling the static function `Project.findOne`. If we get an error, we return the error. If the project does not exist, we return a `null` value. If we find the project, we create a `GithubRepo` module and initialize it with a token and a user and assign it to `git`. We then call the `git.commits` function and pass a list of repositories returning a response. If we get an error, we return an error. If we get a valid response, we return the commits.

```
Project.prototype.commits = function(id, callback){
  ProjectSchema.findOne({_id: id}, function(error, project) {
    if (error) return callback(error, null);
    if (project == null) return callback(null, null);

    var git = new GitHubRepo(project.token, project.user);

    git.commits(project.repositories, function(error, response){
      if (error) return callback(error, null);
      return callback(null, response);
    });
  });
};
```

Let's add a new route `commits` to `./lib/routes/github.js`. We attempt to retrieve the commits by calling `Project.commits`. If we get an error we return `500 Internal Server Error`. If no commits are returned we return a `404 Not Found`. If we receive commits we return a `200 OK` response with the commits:

```
exports.commits = function(req, res){
  logger.info('Request.' + req.url);
```

```
    Project.commits(req.params.id, function(error, commits) {
      if (error) return res.json(500, 'Internal Server Error');
      if (commits == null) return res.json(404, 'Not Found');
      return res.json(200, commits);
    });
  };
```

Now, add the following route to `./lib/express/index.js`:

```
app.get('/project/:id/commits', github.commits);
```

Feature: List issues

```
As a vision user
I want to see a list of multiple repository issues in real time
So that I can review and fix issues
```

Let's add a test to `./test/project.js` for our `List issues` feature. This resource will GET all projects from the route `project/:id/issues` and return a `200 OK` response:

```
describe('when requesting an available resource
  /project/:id/issues', function(){
  it('should respond with 200', function(done){
    this.timeout(5000);
    request(app)
    .get('/project/' + id + '/issues')
    .expect('Content-Type', /json/)
    .expect(200)
    .end(function (err, res) {
      var issue = _.first(JSON.parse(res.text))
      assert(_.has(issue, 'title'));
      assert(_.has(issue, 'state'));
      assert(_.has(issue, 'updated_at'));
      assert(_.has(issue, 'login'));
      assert(_.has(issue, 'avatar_url'));
      assert(_.has(issue, 'ago'));
      assert(_.has(issue, 'repository'));
      done();
    });
  });
});
```

Let's implement the feature `List issues` and add it to our new `GitHubRepo` module `./lib/github/index.js`. We start by defining our function `issues` which takes a list of `repos`. We use `async.each` to loop though all `repositories`.

We then call `github.repos.repoIssues` and we pass our GitHub `user` and `repo`, calling the callback if `github.repos.repoIssues()` returns an `error`. If we get a valid response we use the `map` function to create a new array of items using `underscore pick` function to select four attributes, including `id`, `title`, `state`, and `updated_at`. If the item has a user, we use underscores `extend` function and add the users `login` and `avatar_url`. We then return the items to the main function via `callback` and use the `underscore sort` function to sort the items by date. We then select the top 10 issues and return the issues via `callback`.

```
GitHubRepo.prototype.issues = function(repos, callback) {
  var me = this;
  var items = [];

  async.each(repos, function(repo, callback) {
    me.github.issues.repoIssues({ user: me.user,
      repo: repo }, function(error, response) {
      if (error) return callback();
      if (response == null) return callback();

      var repoItems = response.map(function(model) {
        var item = _.pick(model, ['title', 'state',
          'updated_at']);
        if (model.user) _.extend(item, _.pick(model.user,
          ['login', 'avatar_url']));
        item.ago = moment(item.updated_at).fromNow();
        item.repository = repo;
        return item;
      });

      items = _.union(items, repoItems);
      callback(null, items );
    });
  }
  , function(error) {
    var top = _.chain(items)
    .sortBy(function(item){ return item.updated_at; })
    .reverse()
    .first(10)
    .value();
```

```
    callback(error, top);
  });
};
```

Let's add an `issues` function to `./lib/project/index.js`. We start by defining a function called `issues`. We attempt to retrieve the project by calling the static function `Project.findOne`. If we get an error, we return the `error`. If the project does not exist, we return a `null` value. If we find the project, we create a `GitHubRepo` module and initialize it with a `token` and a `user`, and assign it to `git`. We then call `git.issues`, passing a list of repositories, returning a response. If we get an error, we return an `error` and if we get a valid response, we return the issues and a `200 OK` response:

```
exports.issues = function(req, res){
  logger.info('Request.' + req.url);

  Project.findOne({_id: req.params.id}, function(error, project) {
    if (error) return res.json(500, 'Internal Server Error');
    if (project == null) return res.json(404, 'Page Not Found');

    var git = new GitHubRepo(project.token, project.user);

    git.issues(project.repositories, function(error, response){
      if (error) return res.json(500, 'Internal Server Error');
      return res.json(200, response);
    });
  });
};
```

Let's add a new route, `issues`, to `./lib/routes/github.js`. We attempt to retrieve the issues by calling `Project.issues`. If we get an error we return `500 Internal Server Error`. If no issues are returned we return a `404 Not Found` response, and if we receive issues we return a `200 OK` response with the issues:

```
exports.issues = function(req, res){
  logger.info('Request.' + req.url);

  Project.issues(req.params.id, function(error, issues) {
    if (error) return res.json(500, 'Internal Server Error');
    if (issues == null) return res.json(404, 'Not Found');
    return res.json(200, issues);
  });
};
```

Now, add the following route to `./lib/express/index.js`:

```
app.get('/project/:id/issues', github.issues);
```

Validating parameters with param middleware

You will have noticed that we have repeated the id validation in each of our routes. Let's improve things using app.params.

Here is the offending line of code that simply checks to see if our id is a valid MongoDB id:

```
if (req.params.id.match(/^[0-9a-fA-F]{24}$/) == null)
   return res.json(400, 'Bad Request');
```

Let's add a middleware to handle this ./lib/middleware/id.js. We define a validate function that takes four parameters, with the last being the value of id. We then validate the id parameter, returning a 400 Bad Request, if it's invalid. We then call next(), which calls the next middleware in our Express stack:

```
exports.validate = function(req, res, next, id){
   if (id.match(/^[0-9a-fA-F]{24}$/) == null)
   return res.json(400, 'Bad Request');
   next();
}
```

Now we can use this id middleware in our Express server. Let's include the param middleware and add this line before the first route so that it applies to all of our routes: ./lib/express/index.js:

```
, id = require('../middleware/id')
..
app.param('id', id.validate);
```

We can now edit our two route modules ./lib/routes/project.js and ./lib/routes/github.js, and remove the offending line of code. The id param will now handle this for all routes.

Route improvements

We now have quite a few routes required in our Express server; let's clean this up. A common pattern in node.js is to include an index file that returns all files in its current directory. We will use require-directory to do this for us:

```
npm install require-directory –save
```

Let's create a new module ./lib/routes/index.js. with the following code:

```
var requireDirectory = require('require-directory');
module.exports = requireDirectory(module, __dirname, ignore);
```

Now, all routes in the `./lib/routes/` folder will be exposed under a single variable, routes:

```
var express = require('express')
  , http = require('http')
  , config = require('../configuration')
  , db = require('../db')
  , routes = require('../routes')
  , notFound = require('../middleware/notFound')
  , id = require('../middleware/id')
  , app = express();

app.use(express.bodyParser());
app.set('port', config.get('express:port'));
app.use(express.logger({ immediate: true, format: 'dev' }));
app.param('id', id.validate);
app.get('/heartbeat', routes.heartbeat.index);
app.get('/project/:id', routes.project.get);
app.get('/project', routes.project.all);
app.post('/project', routes.project.post);
app.put('/project/:id', routes.project.put);
app.del('/project/:id', routes.project.del);
app.get('/project/:id/repos', routes.github.repos);
app.get('/project/:id/commits', routes.github.commits);
app.get('/project/:id/issues', routes.github.issues);
app.use(notFound.index);

http.createServer(app).listen(app.get('port'));
module.exports = app;
```

Summary

We have now completed our Web API. We have implemented a basic MongoDB provider; we are using Mongoose to give us a bit of schema support. We have also made a small improvement to our Express server, cleaning up the routes.

In the next chapter, we will consume this API when we build our client.

3
Templating

We have our Web API in place, so let's turn our attention to the client. In this chapter, we will consume our Web API and present our data using a mixture of both server-side and client-side templating. We will serve a `./views/index.html` masterpage file from the server with Express and use `consolidate.js` and `handlebars.js` for templating. On the client side we will use `backbone.js` and precompiled handlebars templates served directly out of the `./public` folder.

Server-side templating

Up until now our Express server has only served JSON; let's install a couple of modules that will assist us in serving HTML.

`consolidate.js` is a template engine consolidation library that was created to map all of Node's popular templating engines to the Express convention for templating, allowing them to work within Express:

```
npm install consolidate --save
```

`handlebars.js` is an extension to the mustache templating language. Handlebars is a logic-less templating language that keeps view and code separated:

```
npm install handlebars --save
```

In order to be able to serve our handlebar templates, we will have to make some changes to our Express server. Let's change the default template engine to handlebars by setting the `app.engine`:

```
app.engine('html', cons.handlebars);
```

Now register `html` as our view file extension. If we did not set this, we would need to name our view `index.hbs` instead of `index.html`, with `.hbs` being the extension for handlebars templates.

```
app.set('view engine', 'html');
```

Let's create our single page application view; this will be served by our Express server:

```
./views/index.html
```

Next we define the location of our `views` folder and the location of our static files folder; it is here that we will store `components`, for example, CSS and JavaScript files.

```
app.set('views', 'views');
app.use(express.static('public'));
app.use(express.static('public/components'));
```

Now create a folder called `public` and add the following directory structure, so that static resources are served with the subdirectory as prefix, for example, `vision/vision.css`.

```
./public
./public/components
./public/components/vision
```

Feature: Master Page

```
As a vision user
I want the vision application served as a single page
So that I can spend less time waiting for page loads
```

Let's add a test to `./test/home.js` for our feature `Master Page`. This resource will GET our master page from route `./` and return a `200 OK` response. The `Content-Type` of the response should be HTML:

```
    var app = require('../app')
  , request = require('supertest');

describe('vision master page', function(){
  describe('when requesting resource /', function(){
    it('should respond with view', function(done){
      request(app)
        .get('/')
        .expect('Content-Type', /html/)
```

```
      .expect(200, done)
    });
  });
});
```

Let's implement our `Master Page` feature. Let's create a new module that exposes a route `./lib/routes/home.js` and add a new `index` function. We start by defining a route called `index`. We create a view `model` with meta information for a page and then render the view passing the view `model`:

```
exports.index = function(req, res){
  var model = {
    title: 'vision.',
    description: 'a project based dashboard for github',
    author: 'airasoul',
     user: 'Andrew Keig'
  };
  res.render('index', model);
};
```

Let's add a new route to our Express server `./lib/express/index.js`:

```
app.get('/', routes.home.index);
```

Package management with Bower

We will now install the various components that make up our client, namely `Handlebars.js`, `Backbone.js`, and Twitter Bootstrap Version 2 using **Bower**.

Bower is a package manager for the web. A Bower package can contain assets of different types, such as CSS, JavaScript, and images. Let's install Bower globally with the following command:

```
npm install -g bower
```

In Bower, dependencies are listed in a `bower.json` file, similar to Node's `package.json`. Let's create a `./bower.json` file and define our client-side dependencies:

```
{
  "name": "vision",
  "version": "0.0.1",
  "dependencies": {
    "json2": "*",
    "jquery": "*",
    "underscore": "*",
```

```
        "backbone": "*",
        "handlebars": "*",
        "bootstrap": "2.3.2"
    }
}
```

Now create the following Bower configuration file ./.bowerrc, which allows us to define our target directory and the name of our bower.json file:

```
{
    "directory": "public/components",
    "json": "bower.json"
}
```

Run the following command to install all of the dependencies listed in our bower.json file:

bower install

Twitter Bootstrap's assets are stored in the folder specified in the path in the following snippet, so let's add a static middleware to override our Express server. This will keep our paths consistent on the client:

```
app.use('/bootstrap', express.
    static('public/components/bootstrap/docs/assets/css'));
```

Templates

Our master page contains the following sections. In order to facilitate a client-side templating model using backbone.js, we will split up our master page into templates.

Let's create a new folder called ./templates and add the following files:

```
./templates
    projects.hbs
    project-form.hbs
    repositories.hbs
    commits.hbs
    issues.hbs
```

In order to avoid compiling the templates on demand, let's install the grunt task grunt-contrib-handlebars, which will precompile our handlebar templates:

npm install grunt-contrib-handlebars --save-dev

We outline the grunt configuration for our handlebars compilation in the following code; it simply takes as input a template location `templates/*.hbs` and compiles these templates into a single JavaScript file and stores it at `public/components/vision/templates.js`.

```
grunt.loadNpmTasks('grunt-contrib-handlebars');

handlebars: {
  compile: {
    options: {
      namespace: "visiontemplates"
    },
    files: {
      "public/components/vision/templates.js": ["templates/*.hbs"]
    }
  }
},
```

We complete this section by taking a look at the master page template `./views/index.html`. The body contains the following areas: a header, which includes either a `login` button or a `logout` button with a `welcome` message, a `project-list` form, `repository-list`, `commit-list`, and `issue-list`.

```
{{#if user}}
    <p class="navbar-text">welcome {{user}},
    <a href="/logout" class="navbar-link">
      click here to sign out</a>
    </p>
{{else}}
    <a href="/auth/github">
    <img src="/vision/github.png" id='login'>
    </a>
{{/if}}

{{#if user}}
<div class="span3">
    <h2>Projects</h2>
    <ul id="projects-list"  class="nav nav-list"></ul>
    <br/><a id="showForm" class="btn btn-large btn-block btn-
primary" href="#add">Add project</a>
</div>
<div class="span3">
  <h2>Repositories</h2>
    <ul id="repository-list" class="nav inline nav-list"></ul>
```

```
    </div>
    <div class="span3">
      <h2>Commits</h2>
      <ul id="commits-list" class="media-list"></ul>
    </div>
    <div class="span3">
      <h2>Issues</h2>
      <ul id="issues-list" class="media-list"></ul>
    </div>
    {{else}}
    <div class="span12">
      <div class="hero-unit">
        <h1>vision</h1>
        <lead>a real-time multiple repository dashboard for
          GitHub issues and commits</lead>
        <p><small>In order to use vision; please login to
          a valid GitHub Account</small></p>
      </div>
    </div>
    {{/if}}
```

Client-side development with Backbone.js

Backbone.js is a lightweight and very flexible **JavaScript Model View (MV*)** framework that simplifies the building of complex JavaScript applications. It includes some very basic primitives that allow us to decouple our client's model and logic from its view. Backbone supports a **RESTful JSON** interface that ties models/ collections to a RESTful API. Further information on Backbone.js can be found at http://backbonejs.org.

Feature: List projects

Let's build the client for our feature List projects. Each item in the list consists of a project name and an edit and delete button. Clicking on the name will display a list of repositories; clicking on **edit** will display an inline form populated with the models' data, and clicking on **delete** will delete the item from our database. We will return to hook up these three functions later. For now, we will simply display a project list.

What follows is an HTML template ./templates/projects.hbs for a project item; it contains a placeholder {{_id}}, which will be replaced by our Backbone application:

```
<a href="#{{_id}}" data-id="{{_id}}">{{name}}</a>
<button class="delete btn btn-mini btn-primary list-btn">del
</ button>
<button class="edit btn btn-mini btn-primary
  list-btn spacer ">edit e</button>
```

Let's define a skeleton Backbone application with all of its pieces in place: ./public/components/vision/vision.js. We start by defining the Vision namespace; we add to it an outer function called Application, that has a single method called start. Here we instantiate a router and call Backbone.history.start() in order to start the Backbone application. We then call router.navigate('index', true) and navigate to our home page. With this function in place, we instantiate new Vision.Application() and call start().

```
var Vision = Vision || {};

Vision.Application = function(){
    this.start = function(){
        var router = new Vision.Router();
        Backbone.history.start();
        router.navigate('index', true);
    }
};

$(function(){
    var app = new Vision.Application();
    app.start();
});
```

Let's now create the application Router. Generally, Backbone applications only have one of these; a router is the entry point for our application.

First we add a function Router, which extends the Backbone Router type. We add a view for our list of projects called projectListView, and add a routes hash, which defines a single route. The entry point for our application is an empty route mapped to a method called index. The initialize or constructor method is called when the router is instantiated; from here we call a method project, which instantiates a ProjectListView. The index method, which matches the route as defined previously, renders our view by calling projectApplication.render().

```
Vision.Router = Backbone.Router.extend({
    projectListView : "",
```

```
        routes: {
            "" : "index",
        },

        initialize : function(){
          this.project();
        },

        project : function(){
          this.projectListView = new Vision.ProjectListView();
        },

        index : function(){
            this.projectListView.render();
        }
    });
```

Let's implement our `Project` model to support our view. We start by adding a function `Project`, which extends the Backbone `Model` type and includes a hash of default values for the two properties in our model. We override the `idAttribute` parameter in order to accommodate MongoDB identifiers. We will use the MongoDB `_id` as our model identifier; by default Backbone will use `id`. This identifier will be appended to any request Backbone makes to the server, for example, when performing GET, POST, PUT, or DELETE. We already added the API for this model in *Chapter 2, Building a Web API*. The `urlRoot` parameter links this model to the web API route `/project` to return a project.

```
    Vision.Project = Backbone.Model.extend({
        defaults: {
              id : ""
            , name: ""
        },

        idAttribute: "_id",
        urlRoot: '/project'
    });
```

Let's implement a collection; `ProjectList` for our `Project` model. We add a function, `ProjectList`, that extends the Backbone `Collection` type and we specify model type as `Vision.Project`. We add a `url` method which returns our web API route `/project` to return a list of projects. The `initialize` method is called when the collection is instantiated; from here we do our initial `fetch()` to get our projects; thus calls the API `/project`.

```
    Vision.ProjectList = Backbone.Collection.extend({
        model: Vision.Project,
```

```
    url: function () {
        return "/project/";
    },

    initialize: function() {
        this.fetch();
    }
});
```

Before we implement `ProjectListView`, let's create `event_aggregator`; this will allow our views to trigger and bind named events that other views can respond to. We will need to do this in order for `ProjectListView` to inform `RepositoryListView` that it's time to display a `RepositoryList`.

Let's add an `event_aggregator` function to the Backbone view prototype using the `underscore.js` extend method to mix in the Backbone `event` module into our views:

```
Backbone.View.prototype.event_aggregator = _.extend({},
    Backbone.Events);
```

Let's implement a view for our `Project` collection— `ProjectListView`. We start by defining a function `ProjectListView` which extends the Backbone `View` type, and add a `Projects` array for our project list. We assign a DOM element to `el`; an unordered list called `projects-list`. This is the element our view will be inserted into. Backbone will construct an empty `div` tag if you do not assign it to `el`.

The `initialize` method is called when the view is instantiated; here we instantiate a new `ProjectList`, passing our `Projects` array. We then call `collection.on('add')`, which upon fetching data from the API will call the `add` method. The `add` method instantiates `ProjectView`, passing to it a `project` model. We then append `ProjectView` to our DOM element via `$el` and return the view.

```
Vision.ProjectListView = Backbone.View.extend({
    Projects: [],
    el: $("ul#projects-list"),

    initialize: function () {
        this.collection = new Vision.ProjectList(this.Projects);
        this.collection.on('add', this.add, this);
    },

    add: function (project) {
        var projectView = new Vision.ProjectView({
            model: project
        });
```

```
            this.$el.append(projectView.render().el);
            return projectView;
        }
    });
```

We complete this section by implementing a view for a single project—`ProjectView`. We start by defining a function `ProjectView`, which extends the Backbone `View` type, and add a `tagName` and assign `li` to it. This tag will be wrapped around our project view; our DOM element is a `ul` tag.

We then include `viewTemplate` and assign our precompiled handlebars template to it. Although the templates are compiled to a single file — `./vision/templates.js`— we still refer to the template by name; `templates/projects.hbs`. The render method renders the view; we pass the `project` model to our `viewTemplate`, which is then added via `$el` to our DOM element and we return the view:

```
    Vision.ProjectView = Backbone.View.extend({
        tagName: "li",
        viewTemplate:
          visiontemplates["templates/projects.hbs"],

        render: function () {
            var project = this.viewTemplate(this.model.toJSON());
            this.$el.html(project);
            return this;
        }
    });
```

If you go into MongoDB and add the following record to the projects collection in the vision database, when visiting the Vision application in a browser you can see this record in the project list view:

```
    {
        "_id" : ObjectId("525c61bcb89855fc09000018"),
        "created" : ISODate("2013-10-17T22:58:37Z"),
        "name" : "test name",
        "token" : "#TOKEN#",
        "user" : "#USER#"
    }
```

Feature: List repositories

Let's build the client for our feature `List repositories`. Each item in the list consists of a repository name, a short description, and a checkbox; which allows us to add or remove the repository from the project.

What follows is an HTML template `./templates/repositories.hbs` for a repository item:

```
<li>
  <label class="checkbox inline">
  <input id="{{id}}" type="checkbox" {{enabled}} value="{{name}}"><h4
class="media-heading repoItem">{{name}}</h4>
  <small>{{description}}</small>
  </label>
</li>
```

Let's add a `Repository` model. We add a function `Repository` that extends the Backbone `Model` type and add a hash of default values for the four properties in our model. The `enabled` property signifies that a repository is included in the selected project.

```
Vision.Repository = Backbone.Model.extend({
    defaults: {
          id : ""
        , name: ""
        , description: ""
        , enabled: ""
    }
});
```

Let's implement a collection for our `Repository` model. We start by defining a function `RepositoryList`, which extends the Backbone `Collection` type. We add the `projectId` of the selected project, and set the model type as `Vision.Repository`. We then add a `url` method and use the web API route `/project/:id/repos` to get a list of repositories for a project.

The `initialize` method is called when the collection is instantiated; from here, we assign the selected `projectId`. The `parse` method is called when a fetch is performed and will parse the response; here we assign our MongoDB `_id` to the `response.id`.

```
Vision.RepositoryList = Backbone.Collection.extend({
    projectId: '',
    model: Vision.Repository,

    url : function() {
      return '/project/' + this.projectId + '/repos';
    },

    initialize: function(items, item) {
        this.projectId = item.projectId;
    },
```

```
        parse: function( response ) {
            response.id = response._id;
            return response;
        }
    });
```

We now implement a view for a single repository. We add a function, `RepositoryView`, that extends the Backbone `View` type and add a `tagName` and assign `li` to it. This tag will be wrapped around our `RepositoryView` function; our DOM element is a `ul` tag. We include a `viewTemplate` function and assign our precompiled handlebars template `templates/repositories.hbs` to it. The `render` method renders the view; we pass the `repository` model to our `viewTemplate` function, which is then added via `$el` to our DOM element, and we return the view.

```
    Vision.RepositoryView = Backbone.View.extend({
        tagName: "li",
        viewTemplate: visiontemplates["templates/repositories.hbs"],

        render: function () {
            this.$el.html(this.viewTemplate(this.model.toJSON()));
            return this;
        }
    });
```

Let's implement a view for our `RepositoryList` called `RepositoryListView`. We start by defining a function, `RepositoryListView`, that extends the Backbone `View` type and adds a `Repositories` array for our repository list. We add an `initialize` method; if `projectId` is empty we return. A valid `projectId` results in rendering the view; first, we clear the DOM element, and we then assign a new `RepositoryList` function to the views `collection`. We initialize the list with our `Repositories` array and our `projectId`, we then call `fetch` in our collection, and then we call `render` for a successful fetch.

The `render` method uses underscore to loop through the repository collection called `collection.models`, calling `add(item)` for each project. We include an `add` method that instantiates a `RepositoryView` function, passing to it a `repository` model. We then append a rendered `RepositoryView` to our DOM element via `$el` and return the view.

```
    Vision.RepositoryListView = Backbone.View.extend({
        Repositories: [],

        initialize: function (args) {
          if (!args.projectId) return;
          var me = this;
```

```
      this.$el.html('');
      this.collection = new
        Vision.RepositoryList(this.Repositories, {
          projectId : args.projectId
        });
        this.collection.fetch({success: function(){
          me.render();
        }});
    },

    render: function () {
      _.each(this.collection.models, function (item) {
        this.add(item);
      }, this);
    },

    add: function (item) {
      var repositoryView = new Vision.RepositoryView({
        model: item
      });

      this.$el.append(repositoryView.render(this.editMode).el);
      return repositoryView;
    }
  });
```

Let's make a few changes to our `ProjectView` and add a click event when selecting a project. We start by defining an `events` hash with a single event called click a, that calls the `repository` method. The `repository` method grabs `projectId` from our model and then calls the `trigger` method on `event_aggregator` for the event `repository:join`, passing `projectId`. We will listen to this event on `ProjectListView`.

```
      events: {
        "click a" : "repository"
      },

      repository: function() {
        var data = { projectId: this.model.toJSON()._id }
        this.event_aggregator.trigger('repository:join', data);
      },
```

Let's hook up the other side of the previous event and add an event binder to `ProjectListView`. We add an `event_aggregator.bind` statement to our `initialize` method, binding the event `repository:join` to the `repository` method. The `repository` method triggers a `join` event on the router.

```
initialize: function () {
  this.event_aggregator.on('repository:join',
    this.repository, this);
    this.collection = new Vision.ProjectList(this.Projects);
    this.render();
},

repository: function(args){
  this.trigger('join', args);
},
```

Let's complete the picture and change router to listen to the `join` event. We add a `repositoryListView` function to the router and add a `listenTo` event to the `initialize` method that calls the `join` method. The `join` method calls `repository`, which instantiates the `RepositoryListView` function, passing `projectId`.

```
repositoryListView:'',

initialize : function(){
  this.project();
  this.listenTo(this.projectListView , 'join', this.join);
},

join : function(args){
  this.repository(args);
},

repository : function(args){
  this.repositoryListView =
    new Vision.RepositoryListView({ el: 'ul#repository-list',
      projectId: args.projectId });
},
```

Now, when you click on a project item's name in `ProjectView`, `RepositoryListView` is displayed.

Feature: Create a project

Let's add a project form for our feature `Create a project`. It consists of a large **Add project** button, a text box for our project name, and `save` and `cancel` buttons. Clicking on **save** will POST the project to our Express server, whereas, clicking on **cancel** closes the form.

What follows is an HTML template `./templates/project-form.hbs` for a repository item:

```
<form class="form-inline">
  <ul class="errors help"></ul>
  <label>name</label>
  <input class="name" placeholder="project name"
    required="required" value="{{name}}" autofocus />
  <br/><button class="cancel btn btn-mini btn-primary form-
    btn">cancel</button>
  <button class="save btn btn-mini btn-primary form-btn form-
    spacer">save</button>
</form>
```

Let's make a few changes to `router` and wire up a route to our `Add Project` button. `routes` now includes a route called `add`, which calls a method called `add`. We include an `add` method that calls `projectListView.showForm()`, rendering our form:

```
    routes: {
      "" : "index",
      "add" : "add"
    },
    add : function(){
      this.projectListView.showForm();
    }
```

Let's make some changes to `projectListView` and modify the `initialize` method. We bind this view to the `reset`, `add`, and `remove` events of the `collection`. We also add a `showForm` method as called in the preceding code. The method renders a project form by calling `this.add()`, passing `new Vision.Project()`, and calling `add()` on the view returned.

```
initialize: function () {
  this.event_aggregator.on('repository:join', this.repository,
    this);
  this.collection = new Vision.ProjectList(this.Projects);
  this.collection.on('reset', this.render, this);
  this.collection.on('add', this.add, this);
  this.collection.on('remove', this.remove, this);
```

```
  },

  showForm: function () {
    this.add(new Vision.Project()).add();
  }
```

Let's add some validation to our `Project` model so we can validate form input for our project. We add a `validate` method to our `Project` model and validate our `Project` model's name. If validation fails, we return an `errors` array containing error messages. We are actually overriding the `validate` method. `Backbone.js` requires that you override the validate method with your custom validation logic. By default, the method `validate` is also called as part of a `save` call.

```
  validate: function(attrs) {
    var errors = [];
    if (attrs.name === '') errors.push("Please enter a name");
    if (errors.length > 0) return errors;
  }
```

Let's make some changes to `projectView`. We start by adding a new template called `formTemplate`, which displays a form for adding a new project. We add two new events to the `events` hash—a button `save` event and a button `cancel` event.

The `cancel` method, which responds to the cancel event, will get the current `projectId` from our model and check if the `model.isNew`. If it's new we simply remove the `projectView` from our `projectListView`. If its not new, we render our view and also render `repositoryListView` by calling `repository`. We then navigate to the `index` page using `history.navigate`.

The `save` method, which responds to the `save` event, grabs `projectId` from our model and the form data. We then call `model.isValid`, which calls the `validate` method in our project model. Any error returned results in calling `formError`. If the model is valid, we go off and get our selected repositories and assign this to our form. We then attempt to save the form as `Project` with a call to `model.save`. Any error returned results in calling `formError`. A successful save enables us to render the `project` in `ProjectListView`. We also render `RepositoryListView` by calling `repository`. We then navigate to the `index` page using `history.navigate`.

```
  formTemplate: visiontemplates["templates/project-form.hbs"],

  events: {
      "click a" : "repository"
      "click button.save": "save",
      "click button.cancel": "cancel"
  },
```

```
add: function () {
    this.$el.html(this.formTemplate(this.model.toJSON()));
    this.repository();
},

cancel: function () {
    var projectId = this.model.toJSON()._id;

    if (this.model.isNew()) {
      this.remove();
    } else {
      this.render();
      this.repository();
    }

    Backbone.history.navigate('index', true);
},

  save: function (e) {
    e.preventDefault();

    var me = this
    , formData = {}
    , projectId = this.model.toJSON()._id;

    $(e.target).closest("form")
    .find(":input").not("button")
    .each(function () {
      formData[$(this).attr("class")] = $(this).val();
    });

    if (!this.model.isValid()) {
      me.formError(me.model, me.model.validationError, e);
    } else {
      formData.repositories = $('#repository-list')
      .find("input:checkbox:checked")
      .map(function(){
      return $(this).val();
    }).get();
  }

  this.model.save(formData, {
    error: function(model, response) {
      me.formError(model, response, e);
```

```
      },
      success: function(model, response) {
        me.render();
        me.repository();
        Backbone.history.navigate('index', true);
      }
    });
  },

  formError: function(model, errors, e) {
    $(e.target).closest('form').find('.errors').html('');

    _.each(errors, function (error) {
      $(e.target).closest('form').find('.errors')
      .append('<li>' + error + '</li>')
    });
  }
```

You will now be able to complete the form and add a new project.

Feature: Edit a project

Let's add an edit project form for our feature `Edit a project`. It consists of a text box for the project name a save and cancel button. Clicking on **save** will PUT the project to our Express server; clicking on **cancel** closes the form. We will use the same handlebars template we used for adding a project. In order to make `RepositoryListView` editable, we will need to introduce the concept of an edit state. We have called `editMode`.

Let's make some changes to `projectView`. We start by adding a new event `edit` to the `events` hash, which calls an `edit` function. We change our `repository` method by passing a new `arg.editMode` to `event_aggregator`, which will inform our `RepositoryListView` that it is in edit mode.

The `edit` method, which displays our project `formTemplate`, populated with our `project` model data calls the `repository` method with `editMode` set to `false`, informing `RepositoryListView` that it is in edit mode. Finally, we update our `add`, `cancel`, and `save` methods; calls in these methods to the `repository` method should pass {editMode:false}.

```
      Events: {
        ...
          "click button.edit": "edit"
      },
```

```
repository: function(args) {
  var data = { projectId: this.model.toJSON()._id, editMode:
    args.editMode || false }
  ...
},

edit: function () {
  var model = this.model.toJSON();
  this.$el.html(this.formTemplate(model));
  this.repository({editMode:true});
},
```

Let's make some changes to `RepositoryListView`. The `initialize` method will now either enable or disable the form checkboxes based on `editMode` when `collection.fetch` makes a successful request. The `enableForm` function removes the `disabled` tag from our `RepositoryListView` checkbox list. The `disableForm` function adds the `disabled` tag to our `RepositoryListView` checkbox list.

```
initialize: function (args) {
  ...
  this.collection.fetch({ success: function(){
    me.render();
    (args.editMode) ?  me.enableForm() : me.disableForm();
  }});
},

enableForm: function(){
  this.$el.find("input:checkbox").remove('disabled');
},

disableForm: function(){
  this.$el.find("input:checkbox").attr('disabled',
    'disabled');
}
```

Now you will be able to edit your existing projects.

Feature: Delete a project

Let's add a **delete** button to our form for the feature Delete a project.

Let's make a change to ProjectView and add a new event to the events hash, called delete, which calls the delete method. We add a delete method, which destroys the model and removes ProjectView. We then call repository, removing RepositoryListView.

```
events: {
  ...
  "click button.delete": "delete",
},

delete: function () {
  this.model.destroy();
  this.remove();
  this.repository({editMode:false});
},
```

Let's make a change to ProjectListView and add a collection event handler to initialize. The event handler calls the remove method when an item is removed. The remove method grabs the model's attributes and searches the Projects collection, removing the item when finding it.

```
initialize: function () {
  ...
  this.collection.on("remove", this.remove, this);
},

remove: function (removedModel) {
  var removed = removedModel.attributes;

  _.each(this.Projects, function (project) {
    if (_.isEqual(project, removed)) {
      this.Projects.splice(_.indexOf(projects, project), 1);
    }
  });
},
```

You will now be able to delete a project by clicking on the delete button.

Feature: List commits

Let's add a list of commits for the feature `List Commits`. Each item in the list consists of a commit `message`, project `name`, a `date`, and the committer's `username`. The following is a HTML template `./templates/commits.hbs` for a commit item:

```
<a class="pull-left" href="#">
  <img class="media-object" src="{{avatar_url}}"
    style="width:64px; height:64px">
</a>
<div class="media-body">
  <h4 class="media-heading">{{message}}</h4>
  <small>{{repository}}</small>
  <small>{{ago}}</small>
  <br/><small>{{login}}</small>
</div>
```

Let's implement our `Commit` model. We define a function, `Commit`, which extends the Backbone `Model` type, and we include a hash of default values for the properties in our model.

```
Vision.Commit = Backbone.Model.extend({
    defaults: {
        date : '',
        ago: '',
        message : '',
        login : '',
        avatar_url : ''
    }
});
```

Let's implement a collection, `CommitList`, for our `Commit` model. We define a function, `CommitList`, which extends the Backbone `Collection` type. We specify the model type as `Vision.Commit`. We add a `url` method that uses the web API route `/project/:id/commits` to return a list of commits. The `initialize` method is called when the collection is instantiated; from here we assign `projectId`. The `parse` method is called when a fetch is performed and will parse the response. Here we assign our MongoDB `_id` to `response.id`.

```
Vision.CommitList = Backbone.Collection.extend({
    projectId: '',
    model: Vision.Commit,

    url : function() {
      return '/project/' + this.projectId + '/commits';
```

```
    },

    initialize: function(items, item) {
      this.projectId = item.projectId;
    },

    parse: function( response ) {
      response.id = response._id;
      return response;
    }
  });
```

Let's implement a view for our Commit collection. We define a function, CommitListView, which extends the Backbone View type, and adds a Commits array for our commits list. The initialize method is called when the view is instantiated; from here we call create and instantiate a new CommitList, passing our Commits array. We call refresh ,which loops through the Commits collection rendering the view with a call to render. The render method uses underscore to loop through the Commits collection called collection.models by calling add(item) for each commit. The method add instantiates CommitView, passing to it a Commit model, it then appends a rendered CommitView to the DOM element via $el and returns the view.

```
  Vision.CommitListView = Backbone.View.extend({
    Commits: [],

    initialize: function (args) {
      if (!args.projectId) return;
      this.Commits = args.commits || [];
      this.$el.html('');
      this.create(args);
      this.refresh();
    },

    refresh: function(){
      var me = this;

      if (!this.Commits.length) {
        this.collection.fetch({ success: function(){
          me.render();
        }});
      }
    },

    create: function(args) {
```

```
    this.collection = new Vision.CommitList(this.Commits,
      { projectId : args.projectId });
    this.render();
  },

  render: function () {
    _.each(this.collection.models, function (item) {
      this.add(item);
    }, this);
  },

  add: function (item) {
    var commitView = new Vision.CommitView({ model: item });

    this.$el.append(commitView.render().el);
    return commitView;
  }
});
```

We continue by adding a view for a single commit item. We define a function, CommitView, which extends the Backbone View type, and add a tagName and assign li to it. This tag will be wrapped around our commit view; our DOM element is a ul tag. We include viewTemplate and assign our precompiled handlebars template ./templates/commits.hbs to it. The render method renders the view; we pass the commit model to our viewTemplate, which is then added via $el to our DOM element and we return the view.

```
Vision.CommitView = Backbone.View.extend({
    tagName: 'li',
    className: 'media',
    viewTemplate: visiontemplates['templates/commits.hbs'],

    render: function () {
      this.$el.html(this.viewTemplate(this.model.toJSON()));
      return this;
    }
});
```

Let's complete the picture and change our router; we add a CommitListView to the router and call commits inside the join method. The commits method instantiates a CommitListView passing the current projectId and a list of commits.

```
CommitListView:'',

join : function(args){
```

```
    this.repository(args);
    this.commits(args);
},

commits : function(args){
  this.commitListView =
    new Vision.CommitListView({ el: 'ul#commits-list',
      projectId: args.projectId, commits : args.commits});
},
```

Vision will now display a list of commits when selecting a project.

Feature: List issues

Let's build our issues list. Each item in the list simply consists of an issue title, project name, a date, the issuer's username, and its status.

What follows is an HTML template `./templates/issues.hbs` for a issues item:

```
<a class="pull-left" href="#">
  <img class="media-object" src="{{avatar_url}}"
    style="width:64px; height:64px">
</a>
<div class="media-body">
  <h4 class="media-heading">{{title}}</h4>
  <small>{{repository}}</small>
  <small>{{ago}}</small>
  <br/><small>{{login}},<b>{{state}}</b></small>
</div>
```

Let's implement our `Issue` model; we define a function `Issue`, which extends the Backbone `Model` type, and includes a hash of `default` values for the properties in our model.

```
Vision.Issue = Backbone.Model.extend({
  defaults: {
    title : '',
    state : '',
    date : '',
    ago: '',
    login : '',
    avatar_url : ''
  }
});
```

Let's implement a collection called `IssueList` for our `Issue` model. We define a function, `IssueList`, which extends the Backbone `Collection` type, and specifies the model type as `Vision.Issue`. We add a `url` method that uses the web API route `/project/:id/issues` to return a list of issues. The `initialize` method is called when the collection is instantiated; from here we assign the selected `projectId`. The `parse` method is called when a fetch is performed and will parse the response; here we assign our MongoDB `_id` to the `response.id`.

```
Vision.IssueList = Backbone.Collection.extend({
  projectId: '',
  model: Vision.Issue,

  url : function() {
    return '/project/' + this.projectId + '/issues';
  },

  initialize: function(items, item) {
    this.projectId = item.projectId;
  },

  parse: function( response ) {
    response.id = response._id;
    return response;
  }
});
```

Let's implement a view for our `Issue` collection. We define a function, `IssueListView`, which extends the Backbone `View` type, and add an `Issues` array for our issue list. The `initialize` method is called when the `view` is instantiated; from here we call `create` and instantiate a new `IssueList`, passing our `Issues` array. We then call `refresh`, which loops through the `Issues` collection, rendering the view with a call to `render`. The `render` method uses underscore to loop through the `Issues` collection called `collection.models`; and calls `add(item)` for each issue. The method `add` instantiates `IssueView`, passing to it an `Issue` model. We then append a rendered `IssueView` to our DOM element via `$el` and return the view.

```
Vision.IssueListView = Backbone.View.extend({
  Issues: [],

  initialize: function (args) {
    if (!args.projectId) return;
    this.Issues = args.issues || [];
    this.$el.html('');
    this.create(args);
    this.refresh();
```

```
    },

    create: function(args) {
      this.collection = new Vision.IssueList(this.Issues,
        { projectId : args.projectId });
      this.render();
    },

    refresh: function(){
      var me = this;

      if (!this.Issues.length) {
        this.collection.fetch({ success: function(){
          me.render();
        }});
      }
    },

    render: function () {
      _.each(this.collection.models, function (item) {
        this.add(item);
      }, this);
    },

    add: function (item) {
      var issueView = new Vision.IssueView({ model: item });

      this.$el.append(issueView.render().el);
      return issueView;
    }
});
```

We continue by adding a view for a single issue. We define a function, `IssueView`, which extends the Backbone `View` type, and add a `tagName` and assign `li` to it; this tag will be wrapped around our `IssueView` function. Our DOM element is a `ul` tag. We include a `viewTemplate` and assign our precompiled handlebars template `templates/issues.hbs` to it. The `render` method renders the view; we pass the `issue` model to `viewTemplate` which is then added via `$el` to our DOM element and we return the view.

```
Vision.IssueView = Backbone.View.extend({
  tagName: 'li',
  className: 'media',
  viewTemplate: visiontemplates['templates/issues.hbs'],
```

```
  render: function () {
    this.$el.html(this.viewTemplate(this.model.toJSON()));
    return this;
  }
});
```

Let's complete the picture and change our router; we add a `issueListView` to the router and call `issues` inside the `join` method. The `issues` method instantiates `IssueListView`, passing `projectId` and a list of issues.

```
issueListView:'',

join : function(args){
    this.repository(args);
    this.issues(args);
    this.commits(args);
},

issues : function(args){
    this.issueListView = new Vision.IssueListView({ el: '
      ul#issues-list', projectId: args.projectId, issues
        : args.issues});
},
```

Vision will now display a list of issues when selecting a project.

Summary

We have now completed the first part of our client. We have implemented a project list view that allows us to add, update, and remove projects. We have also implemented a repository list view that displays a list of repositories for our access token; these repositories can be assigned to the project. We also display a list of commits and issues for all repositories in our project. In the next chapter, we will display a real-time list of commits and issues using Socket.IO.

4
Real-time Communication

Our application is beginning to take shape. We have a list of projects and a form that allows us to add, delete, and update projects. We are also able to assign repositories to these projects, which allows us to view a list of issues/commits for all repositories in a project. This chapter will guide you through the next phase of our client setup: displaying a list of project repository commits and issues in real time using Redis and Socket.IO.

We would ideally like the application to continue working with Socket.IO/Redis switched off, leaving the application without a real-time element. We will attempt to implement these features with this in mind.

Caching data with Redis

Redis is an extremely fast, open source, in-memory key value store. Redis has a useful Pub/Sub mechanism that we will use to push messages to a Socket.IO subscriber that will emit events to the client.

Visit this website in order to download and install Redis: `http://redis.io/download`.

Once Redis is installed, you can start it with the following command:

```
redis-server
```

In order to start the Redis command-line interface, CLI issues the following command:

```
redis-cli
```

The following commands can be issued from the CLI:

- To monitor activity on Redis:

  ```
  monitor
  ```

- To clear the Redis store:

  ```
  flushall
  ```

- To view all the keys stored in Redis:

  ```
  keys *
  ```

- To get the value of a key:

  ```
  get <key>
  ```

In order to use Redis in our application, install the `node-redis` client, as follows:

```
npm install redis --save
```

Let's configure our application to use Redis by updating the `./lib/config/*.json` config files with the following configuration:

```
"redis": {
  "port": 6379
, "host": "localhost"
}
```

First, we create a simple module, `Redis`, that wraps up the Redis connection `./lib/cache/redis.js`. We start by importing the `redis` module. We define a `Redis` module, which calls `createClient` in order to create a Redis client.

We pull in the Redis configuration data from the preceding:

```
var redis = require('redis')
, config = require('../configuration');

function Redis() {
  this.port = config.get("redis:port");
  this.host = config.get("redis:host");
  this.password = config.get("redis:password");
  this.client = redis.createClient(this.port, this.host);
  if (this.password) this.client.auth(this.password,
    function() {});
}

module.exports = Redis;
```

Let's extend our `Redis` module and create a `Publisher` module that will publish messages using the Redis Pub/Sub feature, `./lib/cache/publisher/index.js`. We start by importing our `Redis` module and use the `util` module to extend the `Redis` module with the `Publisher` module. We then define our `Publisher` module, which includes a `save` function, which saves an object as a string to Redis and a `publish` function, which publishes a message to Redis.

The `Publisher` module is defined as shown in the following code snippet:

```
var Redis = require('../../cache/redis')
  , util = require('util');

util.inherits(Publisher, Redis);

function Publisher() {
  Redis.apply(this, arguments);
};

Redis.prototype.save = function(key, items) {
  this.client.set(key, JSON.stringify(items));
};

Redis.prototype.publish = function(key, items) {
  this.client.publish(key, JSON.stringify(items));
};

module.exports = Publisher;
```

Next, we extend our `Redis` module and create a `Subscriber`. `/lib/cache/subscriber/index.js`, which consumes published messages. We start by importing our `Redis` module and use the `util` module to extend the `Redis` module with the `Subscriber` module. We then define our `Subscriber` module, which includes a `subscribe` function. This allows the user to subscribe to messages on a `key`:

```
var Redis = require('../../cache/redis')
  , util = require('util');

util.inherits(Subscriber, Redis);

function Subscriber() {
  Redis.apply(this, arguments);
};

Subscriber.prototype.subscribe = function(key) {
  this.client.subscribe(key);
};

module.exports = Subscriber;
```

Populating Redis

The `./lib/cache/populate.js` script populates a Redis store with new commits/issues using our preceding modules. We will demonstrate scheduling this script later in the chapter. We start by importing the `Publisher` module, and use `util.inherits` to extend the `Publisher` module with a `Populate` function, giving our `Populate` module the ability to publish messages.

We then define the `Populate` function and add a `run` function, that gets all projects from MongoDB. We use `async.each` to loop through each project, using the projects `user` and `token` to instantiate a `GitHubRepo` module. We then call `git.commits`, passing a list of `repositories`; the response returned is a sorted list of the 10 latest commits. We save the response to Redis using `project._id` as the key. We then publish the `project._id` and `commits`, via the `publish` function to activate a refresh. We then repeat the whole process for `issues`.

```javascript
var async =  require('async')
  , _ =  require('underscore')
  , util = require('util')
  , db = require('../db')
  , Publisher = require('../cache/publisher')
  , GitHubRepo = require('../github')
  , Project = require('../models').model('Project');

util.inherits(Populate, Publisher);

function Populate() {
  Publisher.apply(this, arguments);
};

Populate.prototype.run = function(callback) {
  var me = this;

  Project.find({}, function(error, projects) {
    if (error) callback();
    if (projects == null) callback();

    async.each(projects, function(project, callback) {
      var git = new GitHubRepo(project.token, project.user);

      git.commits(project.repositories, function(error, commits) {
        if (error || !commits) callback();

        me.save('commits:' + project._id, commits);
        me.publish('commits', { projectId : project._id, commits :
          commits});
```

```
        git.issues(project.repositories, function(error, issues) {
          if (error || !issues) callback();

          me.save('issues' + project._id, issues);
          me.publish('issues', { projectId : project._id, issues :
            issues});
        });
      });

      callback(error);
    }
    , function(error) {
      callback(error);
    });
  });
};
module.exports = Populate;
```

Socket.IO

Socket.IO is a real-time application framework that allows for cross-browser, real-time communication between a browser and server.

The lack of browser and server support for the emerging WebSocket standard means we cannot easily achieve real-time communication across browsers. In order to achieve this, Socket.IO supports multiple transport protocols including WebSockets, long polling, XHR, and flashsockets, that function as a fallback mechanism for older browsers. Browsers that do not support WebSockets will simply fall back to a transport protocol they do support.

Socket.IO comes in two parts: a server-side module and a client-side script. Both parts need to be installed in order for our application to support bidirectional duplex communication. Let's install the server piece via NPM:

```
npm install socket.io --save
```

Let's configure our application to use Socket.IO by updating our `./config/*.json` config files with the following configuration:

```
"sockets": {
    "loglevel": 3
  , "pollingduration": 10
  , "browserclientminification" : false
  , "browserclientetag" : false
  , "browserclientgzip" : false
  }
```

The next step is to wire up Socket.IO to Express. Let's create and configure a typical Socket.IO server: `./lib/socket/index.js`. We define our `Socket` module, which accepts a single argument: `server`. We require the `socket.io` module and create a new Socket.IO server, passing our Express-enabled HTTP server to it. We then configure our Socket.IO server by setting sensible values for `log level`, `transports`, and `polling duration`, as defined previously in our config files, and return the Socket.IO server.

```
var config = require('../configuration');

function Socket(server) {
    var socketio = require('socket.io').listen(server);

    if (config.get('sockets:browserclientminification'))
      socketio.enable('browser client minification');
    if (config.get('sockets:browserclientetag'))
      socketio.enable('browser client etag');
    if (config.get('sockets:browserclientgzip'))
      socketio.enable('browser client gzip');
    socketio.set("polling duration",
      config.get('sockets:pollingduration'));
    socketio.set('log level', config.get('sockets:loglevel'));

    socketio.set('transports', [
        'websocket'
        , 'flashsocket'
        , 'htmlfile'
        , 'xhr-polling'
        , 'jsonp-polling'
    ]);

    return socketio;
};

module.exports = Socket;
```

Setting `log level` is useful for debugging. Socket.IO supports the following:

- 0: Error
- 1: Warn
- 2: Info
- 3: Debug and defaults to 3

Further information on configuring Socket.IO can be found at:
`https://github.com/LearnBoost/Socket.IO/wiki/Configuring-Socket.IO`.

Let's now use our Socket.IO server and create a handler for Socket.IO `./lib/socket/handler.js`.

We start by importing the `Socket` module, instantiating it, and passing it an Express-enabled `httpServer` parameter. We create a Redis `Subscriber` module and define a `SocketHandler` function that accepts `httpServer` as input. We set up a Socket.IO handler for the connection event. When ready, this will return the connected socket.

We then subscribe to two Redis channels—`issues` and `commits`—and define a Redis handler for the new message event. This handler broadcasts a channel and a message to clients listening on the channel defined by `message.projectId`.

We define a Socket.IO `subscribe` handler, which allows a client to join or subscribe to events on a given project. We also define a Socket.IO `unsubscribe` handler that allows a client to leave or unsubscribe to events on a given project. We also define an `error` handler on Socket.IO, which logs any errors to `logger`:

```
var http = require('http')
  , logger = require("../logger")
  , Socket = require('../socket')
  , Subscriber = require('../cache/subscriber')
  , subscriber = new Subscriber();

function SocketHandler(httpServer) {

  var socketIo = new Socket(httpServer)

  socketIo.sockets.on('connection', function(socket) {
    subscriber.subscribe("issues");
    subscriber.subscribe("commits");

    subscriber.client.on("message", function (channel, message) {
      socket.broadcast.to(message.projectId).emit(channel,
        JSON.parse(message));
    });

    socket.on('subscribe', function (data) {
      socket.join(data.channel);
    });

    socket.on('unsubscribe', function () {
      var rooms = socketIo.sockets.manager.roomClients[socket.id];
```

```
        for (var room in rooms) {
            if (room.length > 0) {
              room = room.substr(1);
              socket.leave(room);
            }
        }
      });
    });

    socketIo.sockets.on('error', function() {
      logger.error(arguments);
    });
  };

  module.exports = SocketHandler;
```

Now we can wire up Socket.IO to our `./lib/express/index.js` Express server. Let's import the `SocketHandler` module, passing to it an Express server called `httpServer`:

```
, SocketHandler = require('../socket/handler')
..
var httpServer = http.createServer(app).listen(app.get('port'))
socketHandler = new SocketHandler(httpServer);
```

Socket.IO on the client

In order to display these Socket.IO published messages, we need to make some client changes. Let's install the Socket.IO client piece using bower:

bower install socketio-client

Let's make a single change to our `./lib/express/index.js` Express server and simplify the location of our `socket.io-client` using the `static` middleware:

```
app.use('/sockets', express.static(
  'public/components/socket.io-client/dist/'));
```

We will now add the Socket.IO client scripts to `./views/index.html`:

```
<script src="/sockets/socket.io.js"></script>
```

Now we integrate Socket.IO into our backbone piece. Let's update our `Backbone.js` `Router`. The router `initialise` method now accepts `socket` as an argument and contains two Socket.IO event handlers: one for issues which calls the issues method and one for commits which calls the commits method. The join method will now emit an Socket.IO `unsubscribe` event unsubscribing the user from any currently subscribed projects. It will then emit a Socket.IO `subscribe` event which subscribes the user to the newly selected project. The project selected is passed to the join method via the `args` parameter.

```
Vision.Router = Backbone.Router.extend({
  projectListView : '',
  repositoryListView:'',
  issueListView:'',
  commitListView:'',
  socket: null,

  routes: {
    '' : 'index',
    'add' : 'add'
  },

  initialize : function(socket) {
    this.socket = socket;
    this.project();
    this.listenTo(this.projectListView, 'join', this.join);
    this.socket.on('issues', this.issues);
    this.socket.on('commits', this.commits);
  },

  join : function(args) {
    this.repository(args);
    this.issues(args);
    this.commits(args);
    this.socket.emit('unsubscribe');
    this.socket.emit('subscribe', {channel : args.projectId});
  },

  project : function() {
    this.projectListView = new Vision.ProjectListView();
  },

  repository : function(args) {

    this.repositoryListView = new Vision.RepositoryListView(
      {el: 'ul#repository-list', projectId: args.projectId,
        editMode: args.editMode });
```

```
    },
  issues : function(args) {
    this.issueListView = new Vision.IssueListView(
      {el: 'ul#issues-list', projectId: args.projectId,
        issues : args.issues});
  },
  commits : function(args) {
    this.commitListView = new Vision.CommitListView(
      { el: 'ul#commits-list', projectId: args.projectId,
        commits : args.commits});
  },
  index : function(){
    this.projectListView.render();
  },
  add : function(){
    this.projectListView.showForm();
  }
});
```

We now need to pass an instance of our Socket.IO client to our `Router`. We call `io.connect`, create a socket, and pass this into our `Router`.

```
Vision.Application = function() {
  this.start = function() {
    var socketio = io.connect('/');
    var router = new Vision.Router(socketio);
    Backbone.history.start();
    router.navigate('index', true);
  }
};
```

Scheduling Redis population

The only thing that remains is to create a scheduler that polls our Redis `populate` script, `./populate.js`.

First, let's install a scheduler named `node-schedule` via NPM:

```
npm install node-schedule --save
```

We start by importing `node-schedule`, which allows us to do cron-like scheduling. We call `schedule.scheduleJob` every five minutes using `*/5`; however, it will also run as soon as the script starts. We then call `populate.run` to start population:

```
var schedule = require('node-schedule')
  , logger = require('./lib/logger')
  , Populate = require('./lib/cache/populate')
  , populate = new Populate();

schedule.scheduleJob('*/5 * * * *', function() {
  populate.run(function(err) {
    if (err) logger.error('Redis Population error', err);
    if (!err) logger.info('Redis Population complete');
  });
});
```

In order to run the application with real-time updates, open a new terminal and run the following command:

npm start

Now, open another terminal to run the Redis population script.

node populate.js

We configured the previous script to run every five minutes, so go and add some issues/commits to your GitHub project repository in order to see the results.

Summary

Socket.IO and Redis are powerful tools. We have barely scratched the surface of what can be achieved with them. We will revisit Redis and Socket.IO in the following chapters of this book as Redis is also used to scale Express sessions and the Socket. IOs Pub/Sub mechanism.

The next chapter will focus on securing our application when we implement an authentication strategy via GitHub, using Passport, and add SSL support.

5
Security

In this chapter we will authenticate users using a GitHub account and **OAuth 2.0** tokens. This will allow us to secure the site and support multiple users; currently we have a single hardcoded token and user. We will also add HTTPS to our site and explore some other modules that we can use to secure other common security vulnerabilities.

Setting up Passport

Passport is an authentication middleware for node that supports; via plugin; multiple authentication strategies, including Basic Auth, OAuth, and OAuth 2. Passport works by defining a route middleware to be used to authenticate the request.

Let's install Passport:

```
npm install passport --save
```

Passport does not include a GitHub strategy; for this we need to install `passport-github`; a strategy for authenticating with GitHub using the OAuth 2.0 API:

```
npm install passport-github --save
```

Acceptance testing with Cucumber and Zombie.js

OAuth authentication uses a callback mechanism; this is messy to test with an integration-testing tool such as SuperTest; we require something a little more end-to-end.

Cucumber allows teams to describe software behavior in a simple plain text language called **Gherkin**. The process of describing this behavior aids development; the output serves as documentation that can be automated to run as a set of tests. Let's install cucumber:

```
npm install -g cucumber
```

Zombie.js is simple, lightweight framework for doing headless full-stack testing. Let's install Zombie.js:

```
npm install zombie --save-dev
```

Let's automate running Cucumber with a grunt task:

```
npm install grunt-cucumber --save-dev
```

Add the following to our gruntfile ./gruntfile.js. The section files defines the location of our feature files, and options:steps defines the location of our step definitions:

```
cucumberjs: {
  files: 'features',
  options: {
    steps: "features/step_definitions",
      format: "pretty"
  }
},
```

Feature: Authentication

```
As a vision user
I want to be able to authenticate via Github
So that I can view project activity
```

Let's create our first feature file ./features/authentication.feature. The following feature file contains a Feature section, which for the agile among you will know that it defines the story and its value to the business, and a list of scenarios. Our acceptance criteria; written in the Gherkin language.

The following Authenticate feature contains two scenarios, including one to log in, titled User logs in successfully, and one to log out, titled User logs out successfully:

```
Feature: Authentication
As a vision user
I want to be able to authenticate via Github
So that I can view project activity
```

```
Scenario: User logs in successfully
  Given I have a GitHub Account
  When I click the GitHub authentication button
  Then I should be logged in
  And I should see my name and a logout link

Scenario: User logs out successfully
  Given I am logged in to Vision
  When I click the logout button
  Then I should see the GitHub login button
```

Let's run Cucumber using our grunt task:

`grunt cucumberjs`

This will generate the following output:

```
2 scenarios (2 undefined)
7 steps (7 undefined)
You can implement step definitions for undefined steps with these
snippets:
this.Given(/^I have a GitHub Account$/, function(callback) {
  callback.pending();
});

this.When(/^I click the GitHub authentication button$/,
  function(callback) {
  callback.pending();
});

this.Then(/^I should be logged in$/, function(callback) {
  callback.pending();
});

this.Then(/^I should see my name and a logout link$/,
  function(callback) {
  callback.pending();
});

this.Given(/^I am logged in to Vision$/, function(callback) {
  callback.pending();
});
```

```
this.When(/^I click the logout button$/, function(callback) {
  callback.pending();
});

this.Then(/^I should see the GitHub login button$/,
  function(callback) {
  callback.pending();
});
```

From the preceding output, you can see that Cucumber has generated a series of stubbed steps that are set to pending. These steps represent the Given, When, and Then scenarios we defined in our feature file ./features/authentication/authentication.feature.

We can use these steps to implement our Cucumber tests. Let's create a step definition file ./features/step_definitions/authentication/authenticate.js:

```
var steps = function() {
  var Given = When = Then = this.defineStep;
  ..add generated steps here
};

module.exports = steps;
```

Let's run Cucumber using our grunt task:

grunt cucumberjs

We get the following output:

2 scenarios (2 pending)

7 steps (2 pending, 5 skipped)

We are now ready to begin implementing our first scenario.

Scenario: User logs in successfully

Let's begin implementing this scenario. First, we need a GitHub clientId and clientSecret. Visit your GitHub account, click on **Settings** and then **Applications** and again on **Register New Application.** Complete the form by adding the homepage URL and the callback URL (same as our homepage), and a clientId and a clientSecret will be generated.

Let's add these details to our config files ./config/*.json:

```
"auth": {
    "homepage": "http://127.0.0.1:3000"
  , "callback": "http://127.0.0.1:3000/auth/github/callback"
  , "clientId": "5bb691b4ebb5417f4ab9"
  , "clientSecret": "15310740929666983d52808dda32417d733791d0"
}
```

Let's remove the temporary login we set up in *Chapter 2, Building a Web API*, and remove the following line and all code related to it ./lib/routes/project.js:

```
, login = require('../../test/login');
```

We are now ready to implement our GitHub strategy ./lib/github/ authentication.js. We start by defining a function, GitHubAuth; we import the passport and passport-github modules. We instantiate a GitHubStrategy, add it to passport, and pass a clientID, clientSecret, a callbackUrl, and a verify function (all passport strategies require a verify function), that is called when GitHub authenticates passing back an accessToken, refreshToken, and a profile.

Inside this verify function, we have the option of rejecting the user by passing a false out of the callback function. We will accept anyone with a GitHub access token; so simply pass back a user profile; which we create using the profile GitHub passed to us. Within the verify function, we instantiate a GitHubRepo and call updateTokens, which updates their access tokens for use by our Redis cache population.

Our application will support user sessions, so we add two functions to the passport module, that include serializeUser and deserializeUser, which serialize and deserializes the GitHub user profile into and out of a user session:

```
var async = require('async')
, GitHubRepo = require('../github')
, config = require('../configuration');

function GitHubAuth() {
  this.passport = require('passport')
  var GitHubStrategy = require('passport-github').Strategy;

  this.passport.use(new GitHubStrategy({
      clientID     : config.get('auth:clientId'),
      clientSecret : config.get('auth:clientSecret'),
      callbackURL  : config.get('auth:callback')
  },
```

```
function(accessToken, refreshToken, profile, done) {

  var user = {
    id : profile.username,
    displayName : profile.displayName,
    token : accessToken
  };

  var git = new GitHubRepo(user.token, user.id);

  git.updateTokens(function(){
    process.nextTick(function () {
      return done(null, user);
    });
  });
};
));

this.passport.serializeUser(function(user, done) {
  done(null, user);
});

this.passport.deserializeUser(function(user, done) {
  done(null, user);
});
};

module.exports = new GitHubAuth();
```

Let's add an updateTokens function to GitHubRepo, which gets all of a users'
projects and async.each through each one updating its token:

```
GitHubRepo.prototype.updateTokens = function(done) {
  var query = { "user" :  this.user };

  Project.find(query, function(error, projects) {
    if (error) return done();
    if (projects == null) done();

    async.each(projects, function(project, callback) {
      project.token = this.token;

      project.save(function(error, p) {
        callback();
      });
    }
    , function(error) {
```

```
    done();
  });
});
};
```

Let's add configuration to our config files `./config/*.json`, in order to support Express sessions:

```
"session": {
  "secret": "th1$1$a$ecret"
  , "maxAge": null
  , "secure": true
  , "httpOnly": true
}
```

Let's wire up our GitHub strategy to our Express server: `./lib/express/index.js`. The first change we make it to include our new GitHub `authentication` strategy:

```
var gitHubAuth = require('../github/authentication')
```

We create a `cookieParser` middleware and include it just before the `bodyParser` middleware, which will parse the cookie header field and populate `req.cookies`. We pass a `secret`; which is a string used to create a signed cookie enabling the detection of a modified cookie:

```
var cookieParser = express.
  cookieParser(config.get('session:secret'));
app.use(cookieParser);
```

The application will require persistent login sessions, so we will include the connect `session` middleware in our Express server in order to provide session support. We will use the `sessionStore`, which is an in-memory session store. We pass in a `secret` and a value for a cookie `maxAge` (a null value will expire the session on closing the browser), `httpOnly` (disallow client-side JavaScript access to cookies; XSS attacks), and `secure` (send cookies over HTTPS only):

```
app.use(express.bodyParser());
var sessionStore = new express.session.MemoryStore();
app.use(express.session({ store: sessionStore,
  secret: config.get('session:secret'),
  cookie: { secure: config.get('session:secure'),
  httpOnly: config.get('session:httpOnly'),
  maxAge: config.get('session:maxAge') }}));
```

The Passport module requires we call `passport.initialize()` in order to initialize `passport`, and in order to provide session support, we must also call the `passport.session()` middleware; we add both to our Express server:

```
app.use(gitHubAuth.passport.initialize());
app.use(gitHubAuth.passport.session());
```

We now define the first of two routes on our Express server; both use the passport strategy for GitHub. The first route is a login route /auth/github; hitting this route will redirect you to GitHub and try to authenticate. If you are not logged in to GitHub, you will be asked to log in. If you are doing this for the first time, you will be prompted. You will be asked if you would like to grant Vision access. The second route; is the route GitHub will callback when authentication is complete:

```
app.get('/auth/github',
  gitHubAuth.passport.authenticate('github'),routes.auth.login);

app.get('/auth/github/callback',
  gitHubAuth.passport.authenticate('github',
    { failureRedirect: '/' }), routes.auth.callback);
```

We have configured our Express server with a GitHub passport strategy. Let's add the two missing routes to our routes, ./lib/routes/auth.js; one for login and one for the callback as described previously:

```
exports.callback = function(req, res) {
  logger.info('Request.' + req.url);
  res.redirect('/');
};

exports.login = function(req, res){
  logger.info('Request.' + req.url);
};
```

In order to simulate the body of our project form containing a user and token, we will add a middleware that simply adds this data to the form for an authenticated user. We can add the projectForm.addToken middleware to all of our routes easily by using app.all, which will apply this middleware to all routes that follow it.

Let's make a further change to our Express server: ./lib/express/index.js, and clean up our middleware by removing all require statements involving it and using require-directory with an ./lib/middleware/index.js file, as we did with our routes. We can now add this projectForm above all the routes that require authentication:

```
, middleware = require('../middleware')

app.all('*', middleware.projectForm.addToken);
.. all routes below
```

Let's create the `projectForm.addToken` middleware in `./lib/middleware/projectForm.js`. The `AddToken` middleware checks if the request is authenticated via `req.isAuthenticated`; we add `user` and `token` to the request:

```
exports.addToken = function(req, res, next){
  if (req.isAuthenticated()) {
    req.body.user = req.session.passport.user.id;
    req.body.token = req.session.passport.user.token;
    req.user = req.session.passport.user;
  };

  next();
}
```

Now that we have authentication in place, let's remove the hardcoded user in `./lib/routes/home.js`:

```
exports.index = function(req, res){
  var model = {
    title: 'vision.',
    description: 'a project based dashboard for github',
    author: 'airasoul',
    user: req.isAuthenticated() ? req.user.displayName : ''
  };

  res.render('index', model);
};
```

Now when we click on the GitHub logo in our header, we are redirected to GitHub which will ask you to log in. Once you have logged in to GitHub, you must grant access to our Vision application; however, future attempts to log in will not require you to grant access to Vision.

Let's complete our Cucumber steps for login using Zombie.js. `./features/step_definitions/authentication/authenticate.js`. First, we include zombie and and define a `steps` function. Then, we set `silent` and `debug` to enable Zombie.js debugging output. We define `Given = When = Then` as Cucumber steps and add a `Before` step, which runs before each test. From here we instantiate a zombie `Browser`:

```
var Browser = require('zombie')
, assert = require('assert')
S = require('string')
config = require('../../../lib/configuration');

var steps = function() {
  var silent = false;
```

```
    var debug = false;
    var Given = When = Then = this.defineStep;
    var browser = null;
    var me = this;

      this.Before(function(callback) {
        browser = new Browser();
        browser.setMaxListeners(20);
        setTimeout(callback(), 5000);
      });
};

    module.exports = steps;
```

The step `I have a GitHub Account` uses the zombie browser to visit the GitHub login page, and waits for the page to load and fill in the login details; we then click on the sign in button:

```
this.Given(/^I have a GitHub Account$/, function(callback) {
    browser.visit('https://github.com/login',
      {silent: silent, debug: debug});

    browser.wait(function(){
      browser
        .fill('login', '#LOGIN#')
        .fill('password', '#PASSWORD#')
        .pressButton('Sign in', function() {
          callback();
      });
    });
});
```

The step `I click the GitHub authentication button` uses the zombie browser to visit the GitHub login page and waits for the page to load and fill in the login details; we then click on the sign in button:

```
this.When(/^I click the GitHub authentication button$/,
    function(callback) {
      browser.visit(config.get('auth:homepage'),
      {silent: silent, debug: debug});

      browser.wait(function(){
        browser
          .clickLink('#login', function() {
            callback();
```

```
            });
        });
    });
```

The step `I should be logged in` uses the zombie browser to visit the GitHub login page and waits for the page to load and fill in the login details; we then click on the sign in button:

```
this.Then(/^I should be logged in$/, function(callback) {
  assert.ok(browser.success);
  callback();
});
```

The step `I should see my name and a logout link` uses the zombie browser to visit the GitHub login page and waits for the page to load and fill in the login details; we then click on the sign in button:

```
this.Then(/^I should see my name and a logout link$/,
  function(callback) {
  assert.equal(browser.text('#welcome'),
    'welcome Andrew Keig, click here to sign out');
      callback();
});
```

Scenario: User logs out successfully

```
    Given I am logged in to Vision
    When I click the logout button
    Then I should see the GitHub login button
```

Let's add a logout route to our Express server: `./lib/express/index.js`:

```
app.get('/logout', routes.auth.logout);
```

Now add the route to our routes: `./lib/routes/auth.js`:

```
exports.logout = function(req, res){
  logger.info('Request.' + req.url);
  req.logout();
  res.redirect('/');
};
```

Let's complete our Cucumber steps for logout using Zombie.js in `./features/step_definitions/authentication/authenticate.js`

The step `I am logged in to Vision` uses the zombie browser to visit the Vision home page, waits for the page to load, and clicks on the login link:

```
this.Given(/^I am logged in to Vision$/, function(callback) {
  browser.visit(config.get('auth:homepage'),
  {silent: silent, debug: debug});

  browser.wait(function(){
    browser
    .clickLink('#login', function() {
      callback();
    });
  });
});
```

The step `I click the logout button` uses the zombie browser to visit the Vision home page, waits for the page to load, and clicks on the logout link:

```
this.When(/^I click the logout button$/, function(callback) {
  browser.visit(config.get('auth:homepage'),
  {silent: silent, debug: debug});

  browser.wait(function(){
    browser
    .clickLink('#logout', function(err) {
      callback();
    });
  });
});
```

The step `I should see the GitHub login button` checks to see if the browser response returns a `success`, and then checks to see if the GitHub login link is accessible:

```
this.Then(/^I should see the GitHub login button$/,
  function(callback) {
  assert.ok(browser.success);
  var containsLogin =
    S(browser.html('#login')).contains('vision/github.png')
    assert.equal(true, containsLogin);
    callback();
  });
```

Securing our site with HTTPS

In order to make our site secure, we will run the entire application under HTTPS. We will need two files: a PEM encoded SSL certificate `./lib/secure/cert.pem`, and a private key `./lib/secure/key.pem`. In order to create an SSL certificate, we first need to generate a private key and a certificate signing request (CSR). For development purposes, we will create a self-signed certificate. Run the following commands:

```
cd ../vision/lib/secure
openssl req -newkey rsa:2048 -new -nodes -x509 -days 3650 -keyout key.pem
-out cert.pem
```

Upon running the second command, you will enter an interactive prompt to generate a 2048-bit RSA private key and a certificate signing request (CSR). You will need to enter various pieces of information including address details, common name or domain name, company details, and an email address.

Let's add a module, `./lib/express/server.js`, that will create a HTTP server based on the `key`/`cert` we have just created. We import the `https` module, read the `key` and `cert` files from disk, and add them to a options object. Then using the `https` module, we create a server passing in these options:

```
var fs = require('fs')
, https = require('https');

function Server(app){
  var httpsOptions = {
    key: fs.readFileSync('./lib/secure/key.pem'),
      cert: fs.readFileSync('./lib/secure/cert.pem')
  };

  return
    https.createServer(httpsOptions,app).listen(app.get('port'));
}

module.exports = Server;
```

Let's use the `server` from within our Express server `./lib/express/index.js`; remove the line that creates our HTTP server:

```
var httpServer = http.createServer(app).listen(app.get('port'));
```

Replace it with a call to our new HTTPS server:

```
var server = require('./server')(app);
```

Now we need to replace all references to `http://127.0.0.1:3000`; port 3000 with `https://127.0.0.1:8443`; port 8443. Our config file contains two references:

```
"auth": {
    "homepage": "https://127.0.0.1:8443"
  , "callback": "https://127.0.0.1:8443/auth/github/callback"
  , "clientId": "5bb691b4ebb5417f4ab9"
  , "clientSecret": "15310740929666983d52808dda32417d733791d0"
  },
```

We have a further reference in our `backbone.js` script `./public/components/vision.js`. When connecting to our Socket.IO server, we pass a URL `127.0.0.1:3000`. We make another important change here; we pass an options object when connecting to Socket.IO with the setting `secure: true, port: '8443'`:

```
Vision.Application = function(){
  this.start = function(){
    var socketio = io.connect('/', {secure: true, port: '8443'});
    var router = new Vision.Router(socketio);
    Backbone.history.start();
    router.navigate('index', true);
  }
};
```

Sharing Express sessions with Socket.IO

Now that we have session support in place, we can share the session with Socket.IO allowing us to accept or reject the connection based on this session data. Express and Socket.IO do this using a handshake mechanism. When a client connects to the server, the handshake is initiated, which consists of executing an authorization function on Socket.IO. Here, the cookie associated with the handshake request is examined and rejected if invalid. Let's install `session.socket.io`; a module that has wrapped up this process:

```
npm install session.socket.io --save
```

First off, let's change our Express server, `./lib/express/index.js`, and pass to our `SocketHandler` module the `sessionStore` and the `cookieParser`:

```
var socketHandler = new SocketHandler(httpServer, sessionStore,
  cookieParser);
```

The `SocketHandler` module now accepts the parameters `httpServer`, `sessionStore`, and `cookieParser`. The `SocketHandler` will now instantiate a `SessionSockets` module passing `socketIo`, the `sessionStore` module, and the `cookieParser`. We change the `connection` event to listen on the `SessionSockets` module instead of the `socket.Io` module so that we can access the `session`. Now from within the `subscribe` event, we can check to ensure the `session.passport.user` is valid. We call `session.touch` which updates the `maxAge` and `lastAccess` properties of a session:

```
function SocketHandler(httpServer, sessionStore, cookieParser) {
  var socketIo = new Socket(httpServer)
  var sessionSockets = new SessionSockets(socketIo, sessionStore,
    cookieParser);

  sessionSockets.on('connection', function(err, socket, session) {
    subscriber.subscribe("issues");
    subscriber.subscribe("commits");

    subscriber.client.on("message", function (channel, message) {
      socket.broadcast.to(message.projectId)
      .emit(channel, JSON.parse(message));
    });

    socket.on('subscribe', function (data) {
      var user = session ? session.passport.user : null;
      if (!user) return;
      socket.join(data.channel);
      session.touch();
    });
  });

  sessionSockets.on('error', function() {
    logger.error(arguments);
  });
};

module.exports = SocketHandler;
```

Cross-site request forgery

Cross-site request forgery (CRSF) is an attack that tricks the victim into executing malicious actions on a web application in which they are authenticated. Connect/Express comes packaged with a Cross-site request forgery protection middleware. This middleware allows us to ensure that a request to a mutate state is from a valid source. The CRSF middleware creates a token that is stored in the requests session as `_csrf`. A request to our Express server will then need to pass the token in the header field `X-CSRF-Token`.

Let's create a security `./lib/security/index.js` module that adds the `csrf` middleware to our application. We define a function, `Security`, that takes an Express `app` as an argument and removes the middleware when in TEST or COVERAGE mode.

```
var express = require('express');

function Security(app) {
  if (process.env['NODE_ENV'] === "TEST" ||
    process.env['NODE_ENV'] === "COVERAGE") return;

  app.use(express.csrf());
};

module.exports = Security;
```

Let's make a change to our Express server `./lib/express/index.js`. The `crsf` middleware requires session support, so we add the following line below the `session` and `passport` middleware:

```
require('../security')(app);
```

As we are using `backbone.js` that uses jQuery under the hood to make AJAX requests, we will need to make a change to our backbone code `./public/components/vision/vision.js`. We will now override the `Backbone.sync` function, so that all requests through it pass the `X-CSRF-Token` in the header. The `X-CSRF-Token` is pulled from a `meta` tag in the master page:

```
Backbone.sync = (function(original) {
  return function(method, model, options) {
    options.beforeSend = function(xhr) {
      var token = $("meta[name='csrf-token']").attr('content');
      xhr.setRequestHeader('X-CSRF-Token', token);
    };
    original(method, model, options);
  };
}) (Backbone.sync);
```

We now need to pass the `X-CSRF-Token` to our master page via the master page route. The token is stored in the requests session as `_csrf`, in the following code we add the token to `csrftoken` in our view object:

```
exports.index = function(req, res){
  var model = {
    title: 'vision.',
    description: 'a project based dashboard for github',
```

```
        author: 'airasoul',
        user: req.isAuthenticated() ? req.user.displayName : '',
        csrftoken: req.session._csrf
    };

    res.render('index', model);
};
```

The csrftoken is rendered in our master page in a meta tag called csrf-token; the backbone sync method will put it from this meta tag:

```
<meta name="csrf-token" content="{{csrftoken}}">
```

Improving security with HTTP headers and helmet

Helmet is a collection of middleware that implements various security headers for Express; for more information on helmet visit https://npmjs.org/package/helmet.

Helmet supports the following:

- csp (Content Security Policy)
- HSTS (HTTP Strict Transport Security)
- xframe (X-FRAME-OPTIONS)
- iexss (X-XSS-PROTECTION for IE8+)
- contentTypeOptions (X-Content-Type-Options nosniff)
- cacheControl (Cache-Control no-store, no-cache)

Let's extend our security ./lib/security/index.js module, and add helmet security for the previous issues:

```
var express = require('express')
, helmet = require('helmet');

function Security(app) {
  if (process.env['NODE_ENV'] === "TEST" ||
    process.env['NODE_ENV'] === "COVERAGE") return;

  app.use(helmet.xframe());
  app.use(helmet.hsts());
  app.use(helmet.iexss());
  app.use(helmet.contentTypeOptions());
```

```
    app.use(helmet.cacheControl());
    app.use(express.csrf());
};

module.exports = Security;
```

Summary

By default, Express uses in-memory sessions. In the next chapter we will move our sessions to Redis. We will also configure Socket.IO to use Redis and explore some other interesting ways of scaling Express.

6
Scaling

In this chapter we will look at options for scaling Express. Our current solution will not scale beyond a single process/server; introducing a few simple changes will allow us to scale Vision both horizontally and vertically. We will also take a look at an alternative web architecture, and examine how decoupling our application can improve our application and help us scale Express further.

Scaling Express sessions with Redis

Running our Express application with the NODE_ENV set to production will output the following message:

```
NODE_ENV=production npm start
```

```
Warning: connection.session() MemoryStore is not
designed for a production environment, as it will leak
memory, and obviously only work within a single process.
```

The default session store for Express is an in-memory store; tying sessions to a single process does not scale.

Also, if the server crashes then we lose those sessions. If we want to scale the Express application to more than one server, we will need a memory store that is decoupled from the Express application. Express has a couple of optional stores; here we will use Redis via connect-redis. Let's configure the vision application to use Redis as a session store.

```
npm install connect-redis --save
```

We will now make a couple of changes to the Express server `./lib/express/index.js`. We start by bringing in the `Redis` module we previously created, that configures and connects to a Redis server. We instantiate one of these into `redis`. We then require `connect-redis` which returns `RedisStore`.

```
, Redis = require('../cache/redis')
, redis = new Redis()
, RedisStore = require('connect-redis')(express);
```

We have in place an existing `sessionStore` which is configured to use `MemoryStore`:

```
var sessionStore = new express.session.MemoryStore();
```

Let's replace this with our new `RedisStore`:

```
var sessionStore = new RedisStore({client: redis.client});
```

Our application is now ready to use Redis to store sessions. We can monitor Redis session activity via `redis-cli` by running the following commands:

redis-cli

monitor

Scaling Socket.IO with Redis

Socket.IO also uses an in-memory store to store its events. There are a couple of issues with this; the first being that if the server fails we lose those messages stored in memory. The second is if we attempt to scale our application by adding more servers, the Socket.IO in-memory store will be tied to a single server; the servers we add will not know which Socket.IO connections are open on other servers.

We can solve these problems by using the Socket.IO `RedisStore`. We start by requiring a `RedisStore`, which is a `redis` module from the Socket.IO namespace. We can also use the vision `Redis` module to create three redis clients: `pub`, `sub`, and `client`. In order to configure Socket.IO to use the `RedisStore`, we set the Socket.IO `'store'` to a `RedisStore`, which passes `redis`, `pub`, `sub`, and `client` as the arguments.

```
var config = require('../configuration')
, RedisStore = require('socket.io/lib/stores/redis')
, redis   = require('socket.io/node_modules/redis')
, Redis = require('../cache/redis')
, pub     = new Redis().client
, sub     = new Redis().client
, client = new Redis().client;
```

```
function Socket(server) {
    /....

    socketio.set('store', new RedisStore({
      redis     : redis
    , redisPub  : pub
    , redisSub  : sub
    , redisClient : client
    }));

    return socketio;
};
```

Scaling Express horizontally

Our current application architecture has coupled together an API; a consuming web client and a worker which populates a Redis cache. This approach works for many applications and will allow it to scale horizontally with the help of a load balancer.

But let's say for example, we would like our API to support clients other than web, say for example, we introduced a mobile client that used our API; ideally we would like to scale our API in isolation and remove anything related to the web client.

Scaling our worker horizontally would simply mean replicating the same work over and over again, which would be pointless. Later, we will discuss how to scale the worker.

In the rest of this chapter we will outline how to split apart our application in order to scale horizontally. We will use the source code from the `chapter-6` version of the vision application. We will, of course, document anything of interest which is required to achieve our goal. We will create four new projects: `vision-core`, `vision-web`, `vision-api`, and `vision-worker`.

Download the source code for this chapter here:

`https://github.com/AndrewKeig/vision-core`

`https://github.com/AndrewKeig/vision-web`

`https://github.com/AndrewKeig/vision-api`

`https://github.com/AndrewKeig/vision-worker`

vision-core

Our first task is to extract everything that can be shared between the `vision-web`, `vision-api`, and `vision-worker` projects into a new `vision-core` project.

This includes the following sections: `./cache`, `./lib/configuration`, `./lib/db`, `./lib/github`, `./lib/logger`, `./lib/models`, and `./lib/project`.

The `vision-core` project is not an application so we remove everything in the root of the project, including `./app.js` and our `./gruntfile.js`, and add a `./index.js` file, which simply exports all of the functionalities shown:

```
module.exports.redis = require('./lib/cache/redis');
module.exports.publisher = require('./lib/cache/publisher');
module.exports.subscriber = require('./lib/cache/subscriber');
module.exports.configuration = require('./lib/configuration');
module.exports.db = require('./lib/db');
module.exports.github = require('./lib/github');
module.exports.project = require('./lib/project');
module.exports.logger = require('./lib/logger');
module.exports.models = require('./lib/models');
```

In order to share the private `vision-core` project with visions other private projects, we add a GitHub dependency to config: `./config/packge.json`:

```
"dependencies": {
  "vision-core": "git+ssh://git@github.com:AndrewKeig/vision-core.
   git#master",
```

vision-api

Let's create a `vision-api` project which contains the web API. Here we need to reuse everything related to the API that includes the following middleware: `./lib/middleware/id`, `./lib/middleware/notFound`, the routes for `./lib/routes/project`, `./lib/routes/github`, and `./lib/routes/heartbeat`. We also include the config files `./config` and all the tests `./test`.

In order to secure `vision-api`, we will use basic authentication, which uses a username and password to authenticate a user. These credentials are transported in plain text, so you are advised to use HTTPS. We have already shown you how to setup HTTPS, hence, this part will not be repeated. In order to set up basic authentication, we can use the `passport-http`; let's install it:

npm install passport-http --save

We start by adding a username and password to ./config/*.json:

```
"api": {
  "username": "airasoul",
  "password": "1234567890"
}
```

We are now ready to implement an ApiAuth strategy into ./lib/auth/index. js. We start by defining a function, ApiAuth, then we import the passport and passport-http modules. We instantiate a BasicStrategy function and add it to passport, passing a verify function. Inside this verify function, we have the option of rejecting the user by passing false out of the callback. We call findUser and check if username and password are the same as those stored in ./config/*.json.

```
var config = require('vision-core').configuration;

function ApiAuth() {
  this.passport = require('passport');
  var BasicStrategy = require('passport-http').BasicStrategy;

  this.passport.use(new BasicStrategy({
  },
    function(username, password, done) {
      findUser(username, password, function(err, status) {
        return done(null, status);
      })
    }
  ));

  var findUser = function(username, password, callback){
    var usernameOk = config.get('api:username') === username;
    var passwordOk = config.get('api:password') === password;
    callback(null, usernameOk === passwordOk);
  }
};
module.exports = new ApiAuth();
```

The vision-api project will need a new Express server ./express/index.js. We start by requiring config via vision-core. We require the apiAuth module which handles authentication, then we apply the passport basic middleware to all of the routes using app.all. We set session:false as basic authentication is stateless.

```
var express = require('express')
  , http = require('http')
  , config = require('vision-core').configuration
  , db = require('vision-core').db
  , apiAuth = require('../auth')
```

```
    , middleware = require('../middleware')
    , routes = require('../routes')
    , app = express();

app.set('port', config.get('express:port'));
app.use(express.logger({ immediate: true, format: 'dev' }));
app.use(express.bodyParser());
app.use(apiAuth.passport.initialize());
app.use(app.router);

app.all('*', apiAuth.passport.
  authenticate('basic', { session: false }));
app.param('id', middleware.id.validate);
app.get('/heartbeat', routes.heartbeat.index);
app.get('/project/:id', routes.project.get);
app.get('/project', routes.project.all);
app.post('/project', routes.project.post);
app.put('/project/:id', routes.project.put);
app.del('/project/:id', routes.project.del);
app.get('/project/:id/repos', routes.github.repos);
app.get('/project/:id/commits', routes.github.commits);
app.get('/project/:id/issues', routes.github.issues);
app.use(middleware.notFound.index);

http.createServer(app).listen(app.get('port'));
module.exports = app;
```

As we are moving to multiple Express servers to support our application, we will move `vision-api` onto port `3001`. Let's configure this into `./config/*.json`, as shown in the following code:

```
"express": {
   "port": 3001
 }
```

vision-worker

Let's continue and create a new project called `vision-worker`, which consists of two scripts `./populate.js` script and `./lib/cache/populate.js`.

Of course we could scale this worker with something such as **RabbitMQ.** This would allow us to spawn multiple producers and consumers, and from this respect, the solution we have is not optimum. If you are interested in improving this part of the application, please refer to Packt's *Instant RabbitMQ Message Application Development*. This book explains how you can implement a worker pattern with RabbitMQ.

vision-web

Finally, we create a new project called `vision-web` which will include everything related to the web client ; simply include everything from `chapter 6` and remove everything we moved to `core` and reference core from `./package.json`. Our current set of `routes` require some significant changes; now that we have decoupled our service layer into its own repository called `vision-api`. vision-web will no longer make service calls directly into the project and github services; these services now exist in the vision-api project, instead we will call the API services exposed on vision-api.

Let's add the configuration to `./config/*.json` for our `vision-api` project. The `vision-api` project has been configured to run on port `3001` and uses basic authentication for security, so we include the `username` and `password` in the `url`.

```
"api": {
  "url":   "http://airasoul:1234567890@127.0.0.1:3001"
}
```

In order to call services on our `vision-api` project , we will simplify things by using `Request` module. Request is a simple client that allows us to make HTTP requests; lets install it:

```
npm install request --save
```

With our configuration in place, we move onto our project route `./lib/routes/project.js`. Here we simply replace all calls to our Project service with the corresponding calls in vision-api. We start by pulling in the configuration we defined in the code snippet above. Each route constructs a URL using this configuration, we use the Request module to call into the API. We return a response which consists of the `response.statusCode` and the body of the response:

```
var logger = require('vision-core').logger
, S = require('string')
, config = require('vision-core').configuration
, request = require('request')
, api = config.get('api:url');

exports.all = function(req, res){
  logger.info('Request.' + req.url);

  var userId = req.query.user || req.user.id;
  var url = api + '/project?user=' + userId ;

  request.get(url, function (error, response, body) {
    return res.json(response.statusCode, JSON.parse(body));
  });
};
```

```
exports.get = function(req, res){
  logger.info('Request.' + req.url);

  var url = api + '/project/' + req.params.id;

  request.get(url, function (error, response, body) {
    return res.json(response.statusCode, JSON.parse(body));
  });
};

exports.put = function(req, res){
  logger.info('Put.' + req.params.id);

  if (S(req.body.name).isEmpty() )
  return res.json(400, 'Bad Request');

  var url = api + '/project/' + req.params.id;

  request.put(url, { form: req.body },
  function (error, response, body) {
    return res.json(response.statusCode, body);
  });
};

exports.post = function(req, res){
  logger.info('Post.' + req.body.name);

  if (S(req.body.name).isEmpty() )
  return res.json(400, 'Bad Request');

  var url = api + '/project/';

  request.post(url, { form: req.body },
  function (error, response, body) {
    var parsed = JSON.parse(body);
    res.location('/project/' +  parsed._id);
    return res.json(response.statusCode, parsed);
  });
};

exports.del = function(req, res){
  logger.info('Delete.' + req.params.id);

  var url = api + '/project/' + req.params.id;

  request.del(url, function (error, response, body) {
    return res.json(response.statusCode, body);
  });
};
```

Let's repeat the same process for our GitHub route `./lib/routes/github.js`; removing calls to the GitHub service with calls to the corresponding endpoints on our `vision-api` project:

```
var logger = require('vision-core').logger
, config = require('vision-core').configuration
, request = require('request')
, api = config.get('api:url');

exports.repos = function(req, res){
  logger.info('Request.' + req.url);

  var url = api + '/project/' + req.params.id + "/repos";

  request.get(url, function (error, response, body) {
    return res.json(response.statusCode, JSON.parse(body));
  });
};

exports.commits = function(req, res){
  logger.info('Request.' + req.url);

  var url = api + '/project/' + req.params.id + "/commits";

  request.get(url, function (error, response, body) {
    return res.json(response.statusCode, JSON.parse(body));
  });
};

exports.issues = function(req, res){
  logger.info('Request.' + req.url);

  var url = api + '/project/' + req.params.id + "/issues";

  request.get(url, function (error, response, body) {
    return res.json(response.statusCode, JSON.parse(body));
  });
};
```

Lets update our tests `./test/project.js`, `./test/github.js`. We now remove anything Mongoose related with direct calls using `Request` module to vision-api in order to seed test data to MongoDB:

```
beforeEach(function(done){
  var proj = {
    name: "test name"
    , user: login.user
    , token: login.token
    , image: "/img/"
    , repositories    : [ "node-plates" ]
  };
```

```
    var url = api + '/project';

    req.post(url, { form: proj },
      function (error, response, body) {
        id = JSON.parse(body)._id;
        done()
    });
});

afterEach(function(done){
  var url = api + '/project/' + id;

  req.del(url, function (error, response, body) {
    done()
  });
});
```

Vertical scale with Cluster

Our `vision-web` and `vision-api` Express applications currently run in a single thread. In order to scale our application vertically, in order to take advantage of multi-core systems, and provide redundancy in case of failure, we can use the cluster module and spread the load over multiple processes. Lets add the Cluster module to vision-core `./lib/cluster/index.js`:

```
var cluster = require('cluster')
, http = require('http')
, numCPUs = require('os').cpus().length
, logger = require('../logger');

function Cluster() {}

Cluster.prototype.run = function(module){
  if (cluster.isMaster) {
    for (var i = 0; i < numCPUs; i++) {
      cluster.fork();
    }

    cluster.on('exit', function(worker, code, signal) {
      logger.info('Worker ' + worker.process.pid + ' died');
    });
  } else {
   require(module);
  }
}

module.exports = Cluster;
```

Let's export the cluster module out of `vision-core`; by adding the following to `./index.js`:

```
module.exports.cluster = require('./lib/cluster');
```

Let's change our Express application in `vision-web` and `vision-api` `./app.js`, and add a third option for running our application, that is, running with cluster support:

```
switch (process.env['NODE_ENV']) {
  case 'COVERAGE':
    module.exports = require('./lib-cov/express');
    break;
  case 'TEST':
    module.exports = require('./lib/express');
    break;
  default:
    var Cluster = require('vision-core').cluster
    , cluster = new Cluster();
    cluster.run(__dirname + '/lib/express');
    break;
}
```

Balancing load with Hipache

Hipache is a distributed proxy designed to route high volumes of HTTP and WebSocket traffic. Hipache supports dynamic configuration via Redis, so changing the configuration and adding vhosts does not require a restart. Based on the node-http-proxy library, Hipache provides support for load balancing websockets, SSL, dead backend detection, and is clustered for failover. Let's install it:

```
npm install hipache -g
```

Let's setup a host for both `vision-web` and `vision-api` by editing the `hosts` file:

```
sudo nano /private/etc/hosts
```

Add two new entries:

```
127.0.0.1  web.vision.net
127.0.0.1  api.vision.net
```

And then flush the cache for these changes to take effect:

```
dscacheutil -flushcache
```

In order to configure a server, we will need a configuration file for each application we want to load balance. In our case, it is `vision-web` and `vision-api`. Here is the configuration file for `vision-api`, `./config/server.json`. Importantly, we are running `vision-api` on port `8443`. We configure an SSL certificate under the HTTPS section as Hipache will terminate SSL not our Express server:

```
{
    "server": {
        "accessLog": "hipache_access.log",
        "port": 8443,
        "workers": 5,
        "maxSockets": 100,
        "deadBackendTTL": 30,
        "address": ["127.0.0.1"],
        "address6": ["::1"],
        "https": {
            "port": 8443,
            "key": "lib/secure/key.pem",
            "cert": "lib/secure/cert.pem"
        }
    },
    "redisHost": "127.0.0.1",
    "redisPort": 6379,
    "redisDatabase": 0
}
```

Let's make a change to the Express server `./lib/express/server.js`, and return a standard HTTP server when running in production; Hipache will now terminate SSL.

```
function Server(app){
    if (process.env['NODE_ENV'] === "PRODUCTION")
        return http.createServer(app).listen(app.get('port'));

    var httpsOptions = {
        key: fs.readFileSync('./lib/secure/key.pem'),
        cert: fs.readFileSync('./lib/secure/cert.pem')
    };

    return https.createServer(httpsOptions,app).
        listen(app.get('port'));
}
```

We now add Hipache configuration for the `vision-api` `./config/server.json`. Please note that we are running `vision-api` on port `3001`.

```
{
    "server": {
        "accessLog": "hipache_access.log",
        "port": 3001,
        "workers": 5,
        "maxSockets": 100,
        "deadBackendTTL": 30,
        "address": ["127.0.0.1"],
        "address6": ["::1"]
    },
    "redisHost": "127.0.0.1",
    "redisPort": 6379,
    "redisDatabase": 0
}
```

We will need to revisit GitHub and change the urls under `settings/applications/ developer applications/vision` to `https://web.vision.net:8443`.

Let's update the `vision-web` configuration `./config/*.json`, and change the GitHub authentication urls to `web.vision.net`.

```
"auth": {
  "homepage": "https://web.vision.net:8443"
, "callback": "https://web.vision.net:8443/auth/github/callback"
, "clientId": "5bb691b4ebb5417f4ab9"
, "clientSecret": "44c16f4d81c99e1ff5f694a532833298cae10473"
}
```

Let's also update the API `url` configuration in the same set of config files:

```
"api": {
  "url":   "http://airasoul:1234567890@api.vision.net:3001"
}
```

Our final change will allow us to support multiple ports for each application; we will change the port setting in the Express server `./lib/express/index.js`, so that it checks `process.env.PORT` for a port number:

```
app.set('port', process.env.PORT || config.get('express:port'));
```

We now start the process of running our application under a load balancer. In order to start the Hipache load balancer for vision-api, run the following commands:

```
cd vision-web
hipache --config ./config/server.json
```

In order to start the Hipache load balancer for vision-web, we run the following commands:

```
cd vision-api
hipache --config ./config/server.json
```

So, we now have a running Hipache instance for vision-api and another for vision-web. Let's create a vhost in Redis and associate the Hipache instance with a series of servers. Now run the redis command line interface:

```
redis-cli
```

First off, let's get the vision-web application up and running and assign a backend running on port 3003 to web.vision:

```
rpush frontend:web.vision.net web.vision
rpush frontend:web.vision.net http://127.0.0.1:3003
```

Let's review the configuration for web.vision:

```
lrange frontend:web.vision.net 0 -1
```

Let's get the vision-api application up and running and assign a backend running on port 3005 to api.vision:

```
rpush frontend:api.vision.net api.vision
rpush frontend:api.vision.net http://127.0.0.1:3005
```

Let's review the configuration for api.vision:

```
lrange frontend:api.vision.net 0 -1
```

Let's run the application under a load balancer, set the PORT environment variable and set NODE_ENV to production when running npm start:

```
/vision-web/NODE_ENV=production PORT=3003 npm start
/vision-api/NODE_ENV=production PORT=3005 npm start
/vision-worker/npm start
```

We now have a vision application running under a load balancer, go visit `https://web.vision.net:8443`. In order to add more backends to our load balancer, let's start `vision-api` and `vision-web` under another port:

```
/vision-web/NODE_ENV=production PORT=3004 npm start
```

```
/vision-api/NODE_ENV=production PORT=3006 npm start
```

When we run the following commands, the backends running on ports `3004` and `3006` will be added to the load balancer:

```
rpush frontend:web.vision.net http://127.0.0.1:3004
```

```
rpush frontend:api.vision.net http://127.0.0.1:3006
```

Summary

Scaling a Web application is nontrivial. Node; using the cluster module allows us to scale it vertically. Scaling horizontally requires us to reach out to the wider community. In our application we have chosen Hipache; a node based load balancer. In the next chapter we will discuss production-level improvements that we can make to our application when we look at performance and reliability issues.

7
Production

In this chapter we will discuss putting an Express application into production. We start this chapter by making our Express application a bit more robust as we look at handling exceptions. We then take a look at a series of performance improvements we will need to make in order for our application to survive in a production environment.

Error handling, domains, and crash-only design

The Node community has embraced a crash-only design pattern, which simply means this: if you get an uncaught exception, catch it, log it, and restart the process. Crash-only design and domains work quite well as a pattern, particularly if your application is using cluster. Let's make a change to our cluster module, ./lib/cluster/index.js, on vision-core. Here, we include the domain module; instead of simply including our module to run in a cluster, we create a domain and call the run method. We then include a domain-based error handler that logs and then closes the process via process.exit(1). The cluster exit handler will pick this up and fork a new process:

```
var cluster = require('cluster')
, http = require('http')
, numCPUs = require('os').cpus().length
, logger = require('../logger')
, domain = require('domain');

function Cluster() {}

Cluster.prototype.run = function(module) {
  if (cluster.isMaster) {
    for (var i = 0; i < numCPUs; i++) {
```

```
      cluster.fork();
    }

    cluster.on('exit', function(worker, code, signal) {
      logger.info('Worker ' + worker.process.pid + ' died');
      cluster.fork();
    });
  } else {
    var d = domain.create();

    d.on('error', function(err) {
      logger.info('Error ', err);
      process.exit(1);
    });

    d.run(function() {
      require(module);
    });
  }
}

module.exports = Cluster;
```

Redis sessions

The majority of Express applications in production that require session support will probably use Redis, so making Redis performant is quite important. Our Redis client, node-redis, uses a pure JavaScript parser; the node-redis documentation suggests using an alternative module for parsing.

Hiredis is a binding to the official Hiredis C library; it's non-blocking and fast. If you install hiredis, node-redis will use it by default. Let's install Hiredis on vision-core:

```
cd vision-core
npm install hiredis redis --save
```

SSL termination

SSL termination is the term given to the decrypting of a TLS-encrypted (HTTPS) stream into plain text (HTTP). The TLS module in Node core is not as fast as some other technologies used for terminating SSL and is generally not used in production. Our application runs entirely over HTTPS, so TLS performance is vital.

Fortunately, we have options for SSL; we will use `stud`, a network proxy that terminates TLS/SSL connections and forwards the unencrypted traffic to a web server. Stud is built on `libev` and is non-blocking; it is designed to handle tens of thousands of connections efficiently on multicore machines. Let's clone the stud GitHub repository:

```
git clone http://github.com/bumptech/stud.git
```

Now compile stud from source:

```
cd stud
```

```
make
```

```
sudo make install
```

When the installation is complete, we can generate a stud file. Stud comes with a default configuration that we can request via:

```
cd vision-web
```

```
stud --default-config > stud.conf
```

Our stud file, `./vision-web/stud.conf`, requires a couple of important changes for it to work; the `frontend` configuration should be set to port `8443`, and the `backend` configuration should be set to our Hipache load balancer for `vision-web`, which we have hosted on port `3003`. Finally, we set `pem-file`, which is a single PEM file that includes an SSL certificate and private key:

```
# stud(8), The Scalable TLS Unwrapping Daemon's configuration

# Listening address. REQUIRED.
# type: string
# syntax: [HOST]:PORT
frontend = "[127.0.0.1]:8443"

# Upstream server address. REQUIRED.
# type: string
# syntax: [HOST]:PORT.
backend = "[127.0.0.1]:3003"

# SSL x509 certificate file. REQUIRED.
# List multiple certs to use SNI. Certs are used in the order they
# are listed; the last cert listed will be used if none of the others
match
# type: string
pem-file = "lib/secure/vision.pem"

# EOF
```

Now that we have our stud configuration in place, our Hipache load balancer will no longer need to terminate SSL. Let's remove the SSL configuration from our Hipache configuration, `./vision-web/config/server.json`:

```
{
"server": {
    "accessLog": "hipache_access.log",
    "port": 3000,
    "workers": 5,
    "maxSockets": 100,
    "deadBackendTTL": 30,
    "address": ["127.0.0.1"],
    "address6": ["::1"]
},
    "redisHost": "127.0.0.1",
    "redisPort": 6379,
    "redisDatabase": 0
}
```

With our configuration in place, let's create a certificate with a private key as a single PEM file.

Simply copy your `cert.pem` and `key.pem` into a single file called `./lib/secure/vision.pem`; private key first followed by your certificate.

Now, we can run stud in front of our Hipache load balancer; stud will handle SSL and will direct unencrypted traffic to Hipache as follows:

cd vision-web

stud --config=stud.conf

Please run the following set of commands to run our stack behind stud:

/vision-web/hipache --config ./config/server-no-ssl.json

/vision-api/hipache --config ./config/server.json

redis-cli (these may already exist in redis)
rpush frontend:web.vision.net web.vision
rpush frontend:web.vision.net http://127.0.0.1:3003
rpush frontend:api.vision.net api.vision
rpush frontend:api.vision.net http://127.0.0.1:3005

/vision-web/NODE_ENV=production PORT=3003 npm start
/vision-api/NODE_ENV=production PORT=3005 npm start
/vision-worker/npm start

Caching

Our static file requirements are minimal; the only static content we serve would be the components used on the client side of our application. In order to cache our static files/components, let's make a simple change to `vision-web/lib/express/index.js`. We set the `maxAge` property to a week, which we store in config, as follows:

```
app.use(express.static('public',
  { maxAge: config.get('express:staticCache') }));
app.use(express.static('public/components',
  { maxAge: config.get('express:staticCache') }));
app.use('/bootstrap',express.static(
  'public/components/bootstrap/docs/assets/css',
  { maxAge: config.get('express:staticCache') }));
app.use('/sockets',
  express.static('public/components/socket.io-client/dist/',
    { maxAge: config.get('express:staticCache') }));
```

Let's add the config value, `staticCache`, to `vision-web/config/*.json`, as follows:

```
"express": {
  "port": 8443,
  "staticCache" : 6048000000
},
```

Now, when we hit our application, the response headers will have a cache-control header. If you visit the homepage for our application and check the response headers via your browser tools for any of the resources served, you should see:

`Cache-Control:public, max-age = 86400`

Favicon

Lets add a favicon to our application using the `connect.favicon` middleware. From a performance perspective, this has some value as we can cache it. Also, your browser will request a favicon even if one does not exist, and this can result in 404 errors being thrown. We will use the existing `staticCache` config value to set `maxAge` for the favicon. Let's edit the Express server, `/vision-web/lib/express/index.js`, and add the `favicon` middleware:

```
app.set('views', 'views');
app.use(express.favicon('public/components/vision/favicon.ico'),
  { maxAge: config.get('express:staticCache') });
```

Minification

We can improve page load time by minifying our static assets. We will minify our JavaScript and CSS files by installing the following two grunt tasks:

`grunt-contrib-uglify`: This allows you to minify JavaScript files:

npm install grunt-contrib-uglify --save-dev

`grunt-contrib-cssmin`: This allows you to minify CSS files:

npm install grunt-contrib-cssmin --save-dev

Let's add these minification tasks to our grunt file, as follows:

```
grunt.loadNpmTasks('grunt-contrib-uglify');
grunt.loadNpmTasks('grunt-contrib-cssmin');

uglify: {
  dist: {
    files: {
      'public/components/vision/templates.min.js':
      'public/components/vision/templates.js',
      'public/components/vision/vision.min.js':
      'public/components/vision/vision.js',
      'public/components/json2/json2.min.js':
      'public/components/json2/json2.js',
      'public/components/handlebars/handlebars.runtime.min.js':
      'public/components/handlebars/handlebars.runtime.js'
    }
  }
},
cssmin: {
  minify: {
    expand: true,
    src: ['public/components/vision/vision.css'],
    ext: '.min.css'
  }
}
```

Let's run the following commands:

grunt uglify

grunt cssmin

Not all of our JavaScript components have a minified version, so we minify these as well, adding a `.min` version for json2 and handlebars.

Compression

We can improve page load times further by compressing static files. Express includes the `compress` middleware, which will gzip an HTTP response. Let's edit the Express server, `/vision-web/lib/express/index.js`, and add the `compress` middleware, as follows:

```
app.set('views', 'views');
app.use(express.logger({ immediate: true, format: 'dev' }));
app.use(express.compress());
```

If you visit the homepage for our application and check the response headers via your browser tools for all of the resources served, you should see this:

```
Content-Encoding: gzip
```

Logging

The Express server, `./lib/express/index.js`, uses the `logger` middleware for logging. The Express logger should only be used in development. In fact, in a production environment, this will seriously impact performance as console functions are synchronous. Let's change the Express server and switch off logging when in production, as shown in the following code snippet:

```
if (process.env['NODE_ENV'] !== "production")
  app.use(express.logger({ immediate: true, format: 'dev' }));
```

Summary

Express in commercial production environments can look a little different, but for good reason. Many of the tasks Express/Node support can be performed better by other tools. In our application, we have tried to stay on the node stack; we have chosen to use stud to terminate SSL as our entire application runs on SSL. Stud will outperform all in this space, including Nginx and Haproxy. Stud will forward unencrypted responses to Hipache, which balances load. Hipache is based on node-http-proxy; it uses cluster for failover. More importantly, unlike node-http-proxy, it can manage memory, making it a reasonable choice for a load balancer.

Hipache works well, but if it's performance you really seek, Nginx and Haproxy are the de facto tools to reach for. For failover, we are using node's cluster module, which along with domains, makes our application a little more robust.

Our static file requirements are minimal, so we have chosen to serve, cache, compress, and minify our static resources via Express. Any deviation from these minimal requirements will make me reach for either Nginx or Haproxy to deliver statics, or a Content Delivery Network.

We have managed to automate many tasks. Our code coverage is sitting at around 80 percent, running YSlow and PageSpeed on our application produces good results. Ideally, we would like to have driven all our requirements via test, driven some of the smaller code modules with unit tests, and added more acceptance tests using Cucumber. I hope that you have at least managed to get the feel of all these elements and will be able to make your own informed choices about testing.

The Node/Express stack is a great platform for building web applications. Working with full-stack JavaScript is a great development experience. The node community and the thousands of Node module developers make Node a vibrant and interesting space to work in.

Index

Thank you for buying
Advanced Express Web Application Development

About Packt Publishing

Packt, pronounced 'packed', published its first book "*Mastering phpMyAdmin for Effective MySQL Management*" in April 2004 and subsequently continued to specialize in publishing highly focused books on specific technologies and solutions.

Our books and publications share the experiences of your fellow IT professionals in adapting and customizing today's systems, applications, and frameworks. Our solution based books give you the knowledge and power to customize the software and technologies you're using to get the job done. Packt books are more specific and less general than the IT books you have seen in the past. Our unique business model allows us to bring you more focused information, giving you more of what you need to know, and less of what you don't.

Packt is a modern, yet unique publishing company, which focuses on producing quality, cutting-edge books for communities of developers, administrators, and newbies alike. For more information, please visit our website: www.packtpub.com.

About Packt Open Source

In 2010, Packt launched two new brands, Packt Open Source and Packt Enterprise, in order to continue its focus on specialization. This book is part of the Packt Open Source brand, home to books published on software built around Open Source licenses, and offering information to anybody from advanced developers to budding web designers. The Open Source brand also runs Packt's Open Source Royalty Scheme, by which Packt gives a royalty to each Open Source project about whose software a book is sold.

Writing for Packt

We welcome all inquiries from people who are interested in authoring. Book proposals should be sent to author@packtpub.com. If your book idea is still at an early stage and you would like to discuss it first before writing a formal book proposal, contact us; one of our commissioning editors will get in touch with you.

We're not just looking for published authors; if you have strong technical skills but no writing experience, our experienced editors can help you develop a writing career, or simply get some additional reward for your expertise.

Express Web Application Development

ISBN: 978-1-84969-654-8   Paperback: 236 pages

Learn how to develop web applications with the Express framework from starch

1. Exploring all aspects of web development using the Express framework.

2. Starts with the essentials.

3. Expert tips and advice covering all Express topics.

CoffeeScript Programming with jQuery, Rails, and Node.js

ISBN: 978-1-84951-958-8   Paperback: 140 pages

Learn Coffeescript programming with the three most populer web technologies around

1. Learn CoffeeScript, a small and elegant language that compiles to JavaScript and will make your life as a web developer better.

2. Explore the syntax of the language and see how it improves and enhances JavaScript.

3. Build three example applications in CoffeeScript step by step.

Please check **www.PacktPub.com** for information on our titles

Node Cookbook

ISBN: 978-1-84951-718-8   Paperback: 342 pages

Over 50 recipes to master the art of asynchronous
server side JavaScript using Node

1. Packed with practical recipes taking you from
    the basics to extending Node with your
    own modules.

2. Create your own web server to see Node's
    features in action.

3. Work with JSON, XML, web sockets, and make
    the most of asynchronous programming.

Using Node.js for UI Testing

ISBN: 978-1-78216-052-6   Paperback: 146 pages

Learn how to easily automate testing of your web
apps using Node.js, Zomble.js and Mocha

1. Use automated tests to keep your web app rock
    solid and bug-free while you code.

2. Use a headless browser to quickly test your
    web application every time you make a small
    change to it.

3. Use Mocha to describe and test the capabilities
    of your web app.

Please check **www.PacktPub.com** for information on our titles